ESSENTIALS® of

MODERN Chinese History

Edwin Pak-wah Leung, Ph.D.
Professor and Chairman
Department of Asian Studies
Seton Hall University

Research & Education Association
Visit our website at
www.rea.com

Research & Education Association
61 Ethel Road West
Piscataway, New Jersey 08854
E-mail: info@rea.com

THE ESSENTIALS®
OF MODERN CHINESE HISTORY

Printed in the United States of America

Library of Congress Control Number 2005920366

International Standard Book Number 0-87891-458-7

A Fundamental History...
An Essential Guide...

In this authoritative account, Dr. Edwin Pak-wah Leung, a leading professor of Chinese studies, explores different aspects of modern Chinese history by focusing on topical issues in imperialism, war, revolution, communism, and modernization. The result is a comprehensive volume bringing together in detail those topics which will fascinate anyone with an interest in China.

An essential reference in its field, the book provides a wealth of critical historical insight and gives superb coverage of all the main issues. Clear, crisp, and concise, this is the book for anyone who wants to understand modern Chinese history, whether for teaching, studying, or just out of curiosity about the People's Republic of China.

As part of REA's celebrated *Essentials*® series, the *Essentials of Modern Chinese History* is the latest title to join our outstanding library of handy study guides and references. Each compact volume in the *Essentials*® series offers the reader a wealth of knowledge and detail. I believe you will find this book enjoyable, and frankly a resource like no other.

Larry B. Kling
Chief Editor

ABOUT THE AUTHOR

Dr. Edwin Pak-wah Leung is Professor of Asian Studies and Chairman of the Department of Asian Studies at Seton Hall University in South Orange, New Jersey. He is also Director of the Asian Studies Graduate Program and Senior Fellow of the Asia Center at Seton Hall. Professor Leung has taught at the University of California at Santa Barbara, University of Hong Kong, Peking (Beijing) University, Zhejiang University, and Wuhan University. He has also been a research fellow at the University of California at Berkeley, University of California at Los Angeles, Princeton University, the University of Michigan, Columbia University, and the Chinese University of Hong Kong. Dr. Leung has published a number of books, including: *Historical Dictionary of Revolutionary China, 1839-1976* (*Choice* Outstanding Academic Book, 1992); *Political Leaders of Modern China* (2002); *Historical Dictionary of the Chinese Civil War* (2002); *Modern China in Transition* (1995); *Modern Changes in Chinese Diplomacy* (1990); and *Ethnic Compartmentalization and Regional Autonomy in the People's Republic of China* (1982).

CONTENTS

CHAPTER 1

IMPERIAL CHINA AND THE MODERN WORLD

1.1 DYNASTIC RULE

In contrast to modern electoral democracy, dynastic rule in China during the imperial period was legitimized by the concept of the Mandate of Heaven (*tianming*). This concept, which first appeared at the start of the Zhou dynasty (c. 1123-249 B.C.E), was deeply rooted in Chinese tradition and the popular mind; it was the justification both for rulers to maintain their power and for rebels to struggle to topple dynasties. Those in power concerned themselves with perpetuating the heavenly mandate, while those trying to acquire power claimed that they were acting on behalf of Heaven (*tian*). Both legitimacy and the right to revolt, therefore, were based on this concept of the Mandate of Heaven.

In the ideas of Confucius (551-479 B.C.E), the Mandate of Heaven manifested itself only through the acceptance of the ruler by his people. It was Mencius (372-289 B.C.E) who developed the idea of the people's right to rebel against corrupt and evil rulers. Like Confucius, Mencius emphasized that good government was primarily ethical government. The rule of a truly moral king was characterized by his benevolence toward his subjects.

The concept of the Mandate of Heaven was a common and persistent theme amongst most rebel movements throughout the several thousand years of Chinese imperial history. Many rebels made repeated references to Heaven, and their movements often carried banners with such slogans as "Realize the Way for Heaven." As an old Chinese saying observes, the successful rebel becomes king, the loser a mere bandit. Success in overturning a dynasty and establishing a new one was an absolute sign of Heaven's approval. This "change in mandate" was called *geming*, a traditional Confucian term that was adapted in the twentieth century by modern political movements to mean "revolution."

1.2   THE QING DYNASTY AND ITS DECLINE

The Qing dynasty (1644-1912) was the last dynasty to rule China. It was founded by the Manchus, a nomadic Jurched tribe that lived in central Manchuria in northeast China. In the late sixteenth century, a chieftan named Nurhaci (1559-1626) united all the tribes under his leadership. His most important innovation was the creation of a military and administrative organization known as the Banner System, which laid the foundation for the conquest of China in 1644.

In the meantime, in 1636, the Manchus proclaimed the establishment of the Qing (Pure) dynasty in its homeland. Their conquest of China was facilitated by the collapse of the Ming dynasty (1368-1644) and by the chaotic conditions in China brought on by widespread peasant rebellions. With the aid of a Chinese general, Wu Sangui (1612-1678), the Manchus were able to defeat the rebels in northern China and capture the capital of Beijing on June 4, 1644. After several more decades of fighting, the Qing rulers finally consolidated their authority over all of China in 1683, when Taiwan was conquered and the last Ming loyalists were defeated.

The first four Qing emperors — Shunzhi, Kangxi, Yong-zheng, and Qianlong, who ruled from 1644 to 1796 — were capable rulers; China remained strong and prosperous under them. In politics, the Qing continued Ming administrative practices with only a few minor innovations. Besides consolidating their rule over China proper, the early Manchu rulers also expanded Chinese suzerainty over Tibet, Turkestan, Burma, Vietnam, and Nepal. Internally, the years from the 1680s to the 1790s were years of general peace and prosperity, a time that later scholars have called the *Pax Sinica*. Taken as a whole, the first half of the Qing period was one in which the traditional political, economic, and social institutions reached their full maturity, and the economy achieved a high degree of interregional integration, with perhaps even the sprouts of capitalism.

By the start of the nineteenth century, however, the Qing dynasty began to buckle under the weight of increasing internal and external problems. Over the century of the *Pax Sinica*, China experienced a phenomenal rise in population, which created a set of serious political, economic, and social problems, all of which lay the roots for the nineteenth-century crisis. The waning of the dynasty was marked by economic stagnation, bureaucratic inefficiency, widespread corruption, military degeneracy, and mounting popular discontent. The White Lotus Rebellion (1796-1804) began a series of domestic uprisings that lingered throughout the remaining years of the dynasty.

Although the Qing was able to suppress the rebellions, the prestige of the dynasty was severely tarnished and the central government left greatly weakened.

The Qing dynasty's internal problems were exacerbated by external pressures from the West. Not until the early nineteenth century did the West pose any serious threat to the Qing. Led by Great Britain, the Western powers increasingly put pressure on China to open its doors to free trade and diplomatic equality. Qing intransigence and the throne's insistence on suppressing the opium trade fueled misunderstandings and led to the Opium War (1839-1842) — the first confrontation between China and the West.

1.3 FOREIGN RELATIONS

Externally, China's traditional foreign relations were regulated by what is known as the Tributary System, which reflected China's world view and conditioned her relations with other states. By virtue of her cultural excellence, economic affluence, military power, and vast territorial expanse, China stood pre-eminent in Asia for many centuries, and claimed to be the Middle Kingdom on earth — the center of the known civilized world. She insisted that all countries desiring relations with her accept tributary status and a hierarchical system of "international relations" that was perfected during Ming times and survived into the nineteenth century. Essentially, the Tributary System was based on an extension of the Confucian domestic order to the international scene: just as every person in Chinese society had his specific status, so every state in an "international society" had its proper station. China unhesitatingly assumed the position of leadership while the smaller states on her periphery were assigned the status of junior members. Thus, the European term "family of nations" would appear to apply more aptly to this China-centered community of states than to Western international society. The underlying principle of the Tributary System was not equality of states as in the modern West, but inequality of states. There was no recognition of international law or diplomatic exchanges.

In retrospect, the Tributary System made it difficult, if not impossible, for the Chinese to accept Western powers as equal. Following the Napoleonic Wars and the Industrial Revolution, the Western Powers were determined to demand that international relations be conducted according to the law and diplomacy of Europe. Hence, the history of Sino-Western relations in the nineteenth century was one of continuous conflict and confrontation, leading to the ultimate humiliation of China.

Gazebo, Huaching Hot Springs

CHAPTER 2

INVASION OF CHINA BY THE WEST: THE OPIUM WAR

2.1 THE OPIUM TRADE AND BRITISH AGGRESSION

In the late seventh or early eighth century, opium was first introduced to China by the Arab community, but was used chiefly for medicinal purposes. It was not until the 1600s that people began to mix opium with tobacco for smoking, and it became very popular among both the rich and the poor. This increased demand led to increased foreign importation, and by 1729 the selling and smoking of opium were prohibited by the Chinese government. Almost simultaneously, the British conquered India and its various opium plantations, thus monopolizing the opium trade. Despite the restrictions on the sale and usage of opium, China's annual importations of the drug grew rapidly and steadily. For example, between 1800 and 1820, 4,500 chests (approximately 135 pounds to a chest) of opium were imported per year on average. By 1838 and

1839, the annual average importation was increased to almost 40,000 chests. Not only was opium becoming destructive to the Chinese people, but also large amounts of precious metals (particularly silver, used for monetary purposes) were flowing out of China on a continual basis.

The British lead in the opium trade was primarily maintained by the East India Company, which allowed Britain to officially deny responsibility for the importation of opium against the Chinese emperor's wishes. Britain shipped the opium from India to China in East India Company ships that held a clause on their licenses stating the prohibition of transporting opium. However, in 1834 the charter for the East India Company was abolished, and private opium traders became the main source for imports. Without the opium trade, Britain would have suffered a severe trade deficit. In 1836, Britain sold $18 million worth of opium to China against the $17 million worth of Chinese tea and silk it imported. With the end of the East India Company, it was imperative for Britain to maintain the opium trade if only for the sake of its economy. However, this was done completely at the expense of the Chinese economy, which was faltering due to the depletion of silver in circulation.

The initiation of private opium trade increased China's national dependency, thus increasing the presence of foreign traders in Guangzhou (Canton). Guangzhou was the only city in China in which foreign trade could take place, known by most as the Guangzhou system of trade. The Guangzhou system was developed as a response to the Western attempt to open China to trade. This was a highly restricted trade system in which foreigners could only do business in Guangzhou, and the business had to be conducted through Cohong merchants. These Chinese merchants spoke English, and were completely controlled by the Chinese government. Eventually, the merchants became extremely corrupt and made a habit of accepting bribes. The strict Guangzhou system of trade was one of the main sources of frustration for the British merchants and their government.

The abolition of the East India Company's charter led the Chinese authorities to fear that Guangzhou would be over-run by greedy and violent foreign merchants. Earlier, in 1831, China had requested Britain to send a *taipan*, or a head merchant, to Guangzhou to supervise the problematic foreign merchants. In 1834, Lord William John Napier arrived in China to fulfill the position of *taipan*; however, he viewed himself as an imperial representative of the British monarchy and thus expected to be treated as royalty. Lord Napier refused to petition the emperor for an audience, and insisted on going to Beijing himself. Napier's disrespect towards the Chinese emperor resulted in his expulsion from China. Two subsequent representatives were sent and each was expelled from his position as well. The fourth representative, Captain Charles Elliot, approached China with a middle-of-the-road policy that combined confidence and strength with caution and conciliation.

In February 1836, the governor-general, Deng Tingzhen, assumed office in Guangzhou and began to crack down on the opium trade. In order to actively restrict the opium trade, the emperor appointed imperial commissioner Lin Zexu in December 1838 to suppress the Guangzhou opium traffic. Consequently, by 1839 Guangzhou was virtually cleared of all opium traffic, an event that proved itself to be disastrous for British traders. On March 24, 1839, Lin seized a British factory, and held 350 foreigners hostage for six weeks until the British surrendered their opium. Three days after the seizure, Captain Elliot issued a proclamation on behalf of the British government asking all British traders to surrender their opium to Lin. The proclamation officially declared the opium public property of the British government, which set the stage for the conflict that was about to ensue. On June 3, 21,306 chests of opium were collected and destroyed by Commissioner Lin. Elliot immediately urged London to start prompt and vigorous proceedings against China. Nearly 300 firms in London, Manchester, and Liverpool that were connected with the China trade started a campaign for action. The situation turned hostile on July 12, 1839, when English seamen in Kowloon killed a Chinese villager, Lin Weixi, and Elliot refused to turn over the British murderers to the Chinese authorities.

Little more than a month later, on August 26, 1839, most British subjects had sensed the beginning of a war and left Guangzhou for Hong Kong. It was on October 18, 1839, that Lord Palmerston, the British foreign secretary, informed Elliot that the government had decided to send an expeditionary force to blockade Guangzhou and Baihe. This led to the first round of fire between the two powers on November 3, 1839, when a private British trading ship approached the Bogue to resume trading. Ironically, the British fired on this ship and the Chinese navy rose to its defense. Of the twenty-nine Chinese war junks, one was blown to pieces immediately, three were sunk and several more were seriously damaged. War had broken out, and shortly afterward the British-Indian government issued a declaration of war on behalf of the British Crown.

2.2 THE OPIUM WAR (1839-1842) AND ITS IMPACT ON CHINA

The British navy arrived in Guangzhou in June 1840, under the direction of Rear Admiral George Elliot, the cousin of *taipan* representative Captain Elliot. The navy proceeded north of Guangzhou to deliver a letter from Lord Palmerston to the Chinese government, but was fired upon by the Chinese navy, which did not understand the meaning of the white flag of peace. The British went north once again and occupied Zhoushan (Chusan) Island to use as a base. After a failure to deliver the letter to Ningbo on July 10, they sailed on to Baihe where the letter was finally received. The emperor authorized Qishan, a diplomat, to receive Rear Admiral Captain Elliot, and determine what exactly he demanded. The emperor believed that war could be avoided through peaceful negotiations. Qishan persuaded the British navy leaders to return to Guangzhou in order to discuss their demands, which included the cession of Hong Kong and an extraordinary indemnity to cover the loss of the destroyed opium. To intimidate Qishan into accepting these demands, the British attacked the forts at Chuanbi, and reluctantly, Qishan acceded. This agreement became known as the Chuanbi Convention, the results of which were contested by both sides of government; the men who constructed it were subsequently dismissed from their posts. Thus, the war continued.

In February 1841, the British took the Bogue forts, destroyed the Chinese defenses, occupied all the strategic points on the Pearl River, and besieged the city of Guangzhou. Guangzhou authorities offered Captain Elliot a ransom of $6 million to save the city from destruction, and Elliot accepted. On May 27, 1841, an agreement was reached that appeared to end the Opium War. The agreement had the following provisions: (1) China would pay Britain $6 million within one week's time; (2) Chinese troops would withdraw sixty miles outside of Guangzhou within six days; (3) British troops would be evacuated from the Bogue; (4) both sides would exchange prisoners of war; and (5) the question of the cession of Hong Kong would be postponed. With the six-million-dollar ransom paid on May 31, 1841, the British began to withdraw their troops and were attacked by 10,000 livid, nationalistic local people in Guangzhou. Once again, the war resumed.

With the dismissal of Rear Admiral George Elliot for his agreement to the Chuanbi Convention, Sir Henry Pottinger arrived in Macao in August 1841 to take over the British military. Once he arrived, he moved north with ten ships and four steamers, carrying 336 guns and 2,519 men. This military expedition conquered Xiamen (Amoy), Dinghai, and Ningbo by October. In June 1842, they moved on to Wusong, Shanghai, and Zhenjiang. Provincial officials became very alarmed and petitioned the emperor to permit peace negotiations. To further distress the Chinese, Sir Henry Pottinger poised his ships for an attack on Nanjing on August 9, 1842. By August 17, the imperial commissioners accepted the peace terms in principle.

2.3   THE TREATY SYSTEM

On August 29, 1842, China was deeply humiliated by the propositions issued in the Treaty of Nanjing, which marked the opening of China to imperialism and the beginning of the unequal treaties system. The Treaty of Nanjing contained thirteen articles, signed on the *Cornwallis* by Chinese officials at gunpoint. The irony of the treaty is that opium, the primary cause of the war, was not even mentioned, a fact that supported the notion that the clash between East and West, China and Britain, was inevitable. The conditions of the treaty were as follows:

1. An indemnity of $21 million paid to Britain.

2. The abolition of the Cohong monopolistic system of trade.

3. The opening of five ports to trade and residence for British consuls and merchants.

4. The cession of Hong Kong.

5. Equality in correspondence.

6. A fixed tariff.

A supplementary Treaty of the Bogue was signed on October 18, 1843, and outlined some specifics that the Treaty of Nanjing did not cover. For example, import duties were fixed at 13 percent and export duties at 10.75 percent. The Bogue Treaty, also called for extraterritoriality, most-favored-nation treatment, and permission for British warships to anchor at five ports to protect commerce and control British sailors. The Chinese government was completely humiliated.

The magnitude with which the British gained control in China encouraged other nations to follow suit. The American and French governments sought similar treaties with China; the Chinese government, fresh from its defeat in the Opium War, did not turn them away. The Chinese then began to adopt a new strategy of defense: playing off the barbarians against one another. On July 3, 1844, the Americans signed the Treaty of Wanghia, which specifically prohibited the opium trade. The treaty contained some of the same provisions as that with the British, particularly extraterritoriality, most-favored-nation status, and the right to maintain churches and hospitals in five ports. The French received the same privileges in their treaty, the Treaty of Whampoa, which was signed on October 2, 1844. All of the grants that China made to the "barbarians" were made partly out of expediency and partly out of ignorance of international law and national sovereignty.

The three treaties signed by Britain, the United States, and France, respectively, marked the beginning of the treaty system, also known as the series of unequal treaties. The treaties were considered unequal because they imposed upon China's sovereign rights, and systematically legalized Western imperialism. After the signing of the treaties, China was officially opened to the West, and even considered by some to be up for grabs, as it would remain for the next hundred years. The Western idea of free trade and the Chinese contempt for trade could not coexist peacefully, as proven by the eruption of the Opium War.

CHAPTER 3

REBEL FROM WITHIN:
THE TAIPING UPRISING

Southern China was severely affected by the illegal opium trade and the Opium War, and was therefore particularly vulnerable to social uprisings. There also existed social conflict in the area between the native southerners and *hakka*, or guest settlers, who had migrated there during the Southern Song period (1127-1278). The *hakka* people were more independent, daring, and prone to action than were the natives. Their major occupations included farming, charcoal making, and mining. It was from these groups of *hakka* that the revolutionary leaders of the Taiping Uprising recruited their followers.

3.1 HONG XIUQIAN AND THE SOCIETY OF GOD WORSHIPPERS

Among the *hakka* people lived the leader of the Taiping Uprising, Hong Xiuqian. Hong was the third son of a *hakka* farming family, and, as a boy, showed a strong potential for learning. However, he failed the civil service examination four times: in 1828, 1836, 1837, and 1843. After his second failure, he met two Protestant missionaries who handed him a set of nine Christian tracts, but Hong was too upset to pay any attention to them. His third failure severely distressed him, and he fell into a delirium for forty days. During his delirium, he saw a vision of the Heavenly Mother and others, who told him to overcome evil spirits. Neither doctors nor sorcerers could cure Hong of his delusions.

Once Hong emerged from his delusional state, he was a changed man. He was more solemn, friendly, and tolerant — characteristics that were not attributed to his disposition before his delirium. For the next six years, Hong continued to work as a village teacher, and attempted to take the civil service examination for a fourth time. His fourth failure came at a time when many were disgusted with the current regime's handling of foreigners in Guangzhou, which gave Hong a greater revolutionary fervor. One day, Hong's cousin Li Jing-fang visited and convinced Hong to read the nine tracts that the missionaries had given him. Once Hong read the tracts, he decided that they were the key to his previous visions of the heavenly spirits, and soon after he and his family were converted to Christianity. They twisted Christian concepts, believing that "Heavenly Kingdom" meant China, and "God's selected people" were Hong and his countrymen. Because of his belief in Christianity and disapproval of Confucianism, Hong lost his position as teacher in 1844.

As Hong began to spread his limited interpretation of the Bible, using religion to build up a following for the revolutionary cause, his schoolmate Feng Yunshan organized the Society of God Worshippers. This organization soon earned more than 3,000 converts among miners, charcoal-workers, and poor peasants, most of whom were *hakka* people. As the movement expanded, better-educated and wealthier men began to join. In 1850, with its headquarters located in Guangxi province, Hong's following was comprised of over 10,000 people. In June 1850, the Society of God Worshippers were called upon to sell their properties and bring the proceeds to a public treasury to create sustenance for the revolution. Thus, Hong and his associates had completed their secret preparations for the revolution. Official declaration of the revolution took place on January 11, 1851, when Hong was proclaimed the "Heavenly King" of the new "Heavenly Kingdom of Great Peace." He was to be assisted by his associates, later called the East, South, North, West and Assistant Kings.

Taiping control over southern China began to be realized in the next few years. From September 1851 to March 1853, Yongan, Hunan (including the provincial capital Changsha), Yuezhou, Wuhan, and Nanjing were all conquered. In Yongan, which was captured on September 25, 1851, the Taipings set up a new base and increased the army to over 37,000 men. On April 3, 1852, the rebel forces entered Hunan province, with the goal of capturing the capital Changsha, but they suffered two major losses with the deaths of the South King and the West King. In Yuezhou, on December 13, 1852, the Taipings were successful in acquiring a large amount of ammunition and vessels, which fortified them for the move into Wuhan. March 19-21, 1853, marked the capture of Nanjing, a capture that branded the Taiping Uprising a success, and which led to the establishment of the Taiping Heavenly Kingdom.

3.2 THE TAIPING HEAVENLY KINGDOM

The Taiping Heavenly Kingdom was a theocracy in which religion, civil and military administration, culture and society were all interwoven. A definite puritanical spirit emerged in the early period of the Taipings, in which opium smoking, the use of tobacco and wine, prostitution, footbinding, sale of slaves, gambling, and polygamy were all prohibited. The Taipings wore their hair long, which was quite the opposite of Manchu traditions. A Taiping constitution entitled, "The Land System of the Heavenly Kingdom," was drawn to cover all aspects of military, civil, financial, judicial, and educational institutions, not just the new land system. Overall, Taiping society was a marked contrast to Qing society. Some of its institutions and policies were as follows:

Land Reform began with the abolition of private ownership of land and property. A Taiping proclamation was issued that stated all children of God must be free from want, must have land to till, rice to eat, clothes to wear, and money to spend. The land was divided into nine classes according to yield, and all men and women over sixteen received a share of the land. The distributed land was not the property of the recipients, since they were merely given the right to use it for production. Savings of surplus and private property was prohibited.

The Unity of Military and Civil Administration was very unusual. Soldiers were farmers, and officers were assigned civil as well as military duties. When more families were formed, new army units were organized. Every twenty-five families formed the basic social unit, under the charge of a master sergeant. Affairs such as marriages and funerals were paid for out of a public storehouse.

The Unity of Culture and Religion was a primary factor underlying the Taiping institutionalization. First and foremost, the inculcation of Christian ideas among the Taiping people was a priority of the new government. The Taipings held their own civil service examinations, which were based on selections from the Bible, Christian tracts,

18

and Taiping proclamations. The exams were not as rigorous as those of the Qing, and almost 800 out of every 1,000 candidates passed.

The New Calendar created by the Taipings was neither lunar nor solar, but somewhere in between. The year was divided into 366 days, with 31 days to each odd month, and 30 days to each even month. The problem with this calendar was that it created three superfluous days every four years, or thirty extra days every forty years. This was counteracted by the creation of a catch-up year, designed to regulate the spillovers from the preceding years.

The Social Policies of the Taiping Heavenly Kingdom were very progressive in terms of gender. Men and women were considered equal, and women were even allowed to serve in the civil and military administration. Social welfare measures were taken to support the disabled, sick, widowed, and orphaned.

3.3 SUPPRESSION OF THE TAIPINGS BY THE QING GOVERNMENT

In order to suppress the rebellion, the Qing government was forced to resort to organizing a militia for local defense. The Taiping conquest of Changsha in Hunan prompted the court to order the scholar-official Zeng Guofan to organize the defense of his home province. Zeng was a persistent, brilliant scholar, who was most known for his tenacity of purpose and cool-headedness in emergencies. Zeng knew that he had to go beyond imperial orders and raise a new army in order to be effective against the Taipings. His army's mission was to defend the Chinese cultural heritage in the traditions of Confucius and Mencius. Although Zeng initially raised three battalions of troops, which totaled 1,080 men, he gradually expanded his following. Thus, in February of 1854, Zeng set out for Hubei province with a force of over 17,000 men.

On May 1, 1854, Zeng's troops scored a major victory at Xiangtan. Their success continued into the fall, when they reclaimed Wuchang in October. With confidence, Zeng's troops — also known as the Hunan army — entered Jiangxi but only got themselves into trouble. The Taipings managed to retake Wuchang again in April 1855, and subsequently, Hubei and Jiangxi. With the recapture of these areas, the entire Yangzi valley fell to the revolutionaries, whose success was short-lived due to their fall from within. The Taipings became weak after their East King, Yang Xiuqing, sought to challenge Hong's power. Meanwhile, in 1860, the Qing's defense gained fervor with the official designation of Zeng as imperial commissioner and governor-general of Liang-Jiang. Moreover, Zeng's brother, Zeng Guoqian, claimed the important city of Anqing and the tide was turned in favor of the Qing. This led the imperial court into a new round of attempts aimed at recovering cities along the Yangzi River.

Zeng Guoqian was soon assigned the important task of reclaiming the capital, Nanjing. In June 1862, he penetrated the vicinity of the capital, and with 20,000 men he began a long siege of the Heavenly Kingdom. At this time, foreigners were no longer sympathetic to the Taiping cause, and realized that their interests would be better served with the reinstatement of Manchu rule. By November 1863, the whole province of Jiangsu was pacified, except for Nanjing and a few small pockets. This enabled the Qing forces to cut off the supplies headed to the Heavenly Kingdom, which further weakened Taiping control. Due to the turn of events, on June 1, 1864, Hong Xiuqian committed suicide. His son was set to replace him as the "Young Heavenly King," but was forced to flee the city on July 19, when Zeng Guoqian charged into the city and carried out a merciless massacre. The Qing government issued a standing order that all of the Taipings who surrendered should be decapitated. The Young Heavenly King managed to flee the kingdom, but was discovered in another village and executed. With his execution, the uprising came to an end in 1864. The suppression of the Taiping Uprising reversed the downward course of the dynasty and gave way to a restoration. The Uprising had affected sixteen of the eighteen provinces in China proper and had lasted for fourteen years.

Detail of Beijing Palace

CHAPTER 4

CHINA'S EARLY MODERNIZATION

4.1 FROM RESTORATION TO MODERNIZATION: THE LEADERS

The suppression of the Taiping Uprising in 1864, together with an earlier peace settlement with Britain and France in 1860, eliminated an internal and external threat to the Qing Dynasty, thus paving the way for a period of resurgence. This period constituted the restoration of traditional order and the Confucian government, the maintenance of peace with foreign powers, and the initiation of the Self-Strengthening Movement for modernization. Within the bureaucracy, stricter discipline was enforced and cases of corruption were punished. Emperor Tongzhi (r.1862-1874) was a minor power during eleven of his thirteen reigning years and a weakling in the remaining two. Due to his weakness, the power of the state was grasped firmly by the Empress Dowager Cixi. Henceforth, the emperor was more an institution than a personality.

Prince Gong, another influential imperial official, had been left in Beijing to deal with Lord Elgin and Baron Gros in September 1860 when Emperor Xianfeng (r. 1851-1861) fled to Rehe in the face of an advancing foreign enemy. His departure led to the emergence of Prince Gong as a new and powerful leader. Emperor Xianfeng continued to reject the possibility of returning to Beijing simply because he was so ashamed of his unheroic flight out of the city. Prince Gong finally convinced him to return in February 1861; however, his failing health resulted in a cancellation. On August 21, 1861, while on his deathbed, Emperor Xianfeng named his son Zaichun the heir apparent. Quickly, the Assistant Grand Secretary Sushun, Prince Yi, and Prince Zheng issued an edict that declared themselves advisors on state affairs and members of the Council of Regents for the boy emperor. Prince Gong, as well as the dowagers Cixi and Cian, were left with nothing, and eagerly joined forces to vie for a shift in power.

Prince Gong and the dowagers soon decided that they would try to arrest the regents in Beijing, where they maintained an upper hand on the power scale. The British played a secret role in supporting Prince Gong, since they knew it was in their best interests to keep him in power. Thus, on October 26, 1861 the dowagers left for Beijing with the boy emperor. Upon their arrival, they were asked to take control of the state administration during the emperor's years of minority. Approximately one day later, the dowagers summoned Prince Gong, the grand secretaries, and other high officials to the palace and announced the crimes of the eight regents and their immediate dismissal. When the Princes Yi and Zheng protested, the dowagers issued a second edict which stripped both them and Assistant Grand Secretary Sushun of their noble status, and placed them in the hands of the Imperial Clan Court for punishment. The two princes were arrested and permitted to hang themselves, while Sushun was decapitated. Consequently,

Prince Gong and the dowagers had become co-regents. This was the palace coup of 1861, which paved the way for the launching of the Self-Strengthening Movement (1861-1895) and the modernization of China.

4.2 THE SELF-STRENGTHENING MOVEMENT (1861-1895)

The majority of self-strengthening projects were promoted by provincial authorities who had learned firsthand the superiority of Western guns and ships. These men included Zeng Guofan, Zuo Zongtang, and Li Hongzhang. Zeng Guofan attempted to construct a steamship in Anqing in 1862-63, but the result was a ship that could not move very fast or freely. He then became more determined to unlock the secrets of shipbuilding and gun making in order to break the Western monopoly of power. Under his sponsorship, the Jiangnan Arsenal, a major accomplishment in the early phase of the Self-Strengthening Movement, was established at Shanghai in 1865. It manufactured guns, cannons, and ships, and maintained a translation bureau. In 1868, its first ship was successfully completed. The second pioneer in the Self-Strengthening Movement was Zuo Zongtang, whose interest in shipbuilding blossomed into the establishment of the Fuzhou Dockyard in 1866. The dockyard produced a total of 40 ships and trained able officers. It is considered to be the second most important achievement in the Self-Strengthening Movement.

The most prominent figure of the Self-Strengthening Movement was Li Hongzhang, who was well known for his awesome power with guns and ships, due to his association with the Ever Victorious Army and with foreign officers. Li had an adoration for the Western military system and believed that China's only hope was to meet the challenge from the West and strengthen itself. With the death of Zeng Guofan in 1872, and the involvement of Zuo Zongtang in the Moslem campaign from 1868-1880, Li became the central spirit of the movement, particularly in the provinces. For thirty years Li was principal architect and instigator of "Foreign Matters," and boasted of achievements such as the Nanjing Arsenal, The Military Academy at Tianjin, and the Beiyang Fleet of 1888. However, Li's downfall was his failure to recognize China's need for political and social reform, rather than only military reform. Conservative Confucian society and officialdom were so ill disposed toward innovations that the Self-Strengtheners had to fight every inch of the way to launch the movement.

FIRST PERIOD (1861-1872)

The first period of the Self-Strengthening Movement stressed the adoption of Western firearms, machines, scientific knowledge, and the training of technical and diplomatic personnel through the establishment of translation bureaus, new schools, and the dispatch of students abroad. Its motivation stemmed from the desire to learn the superior techniques of the barbarians in order to control them. The leaders of the first phase were Prince Gong, Wenxiang, Zeng Guofan, Zuo Zongtang, and Li Hongzhang. A major emphasis was placed upon the development of military industries. Accordingly, the first period gave rise to major military establishments, which included the start-up of a small gun factory at Suzhou; the developments of the Jiangnan Arsenal at Shanghai, the Fuzhou Dockyard, and the Nanjing Arsenal; and the expansion of the Tianjin Machine Factory.

SECOND PERIOD (1872-1885)

During the second period of the Self-Strengthening Movement, the ideas that wealth was the basis of power and that modern defense cost more than traditional defense, gained more recognition. Greater attention was then directed to the development of profit-oriented enterprises such as shipping, railways, mining, and the telegraph. The re-directed attention can be noted by the appearance of another type of enterprise during the second period. This new type of enterprise was government-supervised, merchant undertakings, in which capital was provided by private merchants, but management was in the hands of the government-appointed officials. Foremost among this type of enterprise were the China Merchants' Steam Navigation Company, Kaiping Coal Mines, Shanghai Cotton Cloth Mill, and the Imperial Telegraph Administration. At this point in the reform, Li Hongzhang had earned Empress Dowager's trust, and thus, over 90 percent of the modernization projects were launched under his leadership.

THIRD PERIOD (1885-1895)

The last period of self-strengthening continued to highlight military and naval growth, but the idea of enriching the nation through light industry gained increasing favor. More specifically, the textile and cotton-weaving industries grew tremendously. In Guangzhou, the years during 1886-1889 yielded a textile mill, cotton mill, iron factory, and mint. Other cities in China experienced a growth in light industry during the same interval as well. However, historically rooted jealousy towards merchants caused the failure of private enterprise, and joint government and merchant enterprises. Guizhou Ironworks (1891) and Hubei Textile Company (1894) were both enterprises whose private capital was welcomed, but whose private control was resented.

4.3   THE LEGACIES OF EARLY MODERNIZATION

The Self-Strengthening Movement is best characterized by superficial attempts to modernize, but it was limited in its scope of activity. There were no attempts to assimilate Western institutions, philosophy, arts, and culture. The weakness of the reform movement was exposed in the Sino-French War of 1884-1885, when China was unable to defend its tributary state, Annam (Vietnam). It was further confirmed by China's defeat in the Sino-Japanese War of 1894-1895. There were several factors that contributed to the failure of the Self-Strengthening Movement that included, but were not limited to, the following:

(1) *Lack of coordination:* During the period in which the Self-Strengthening Movement took place, there was no strong central government. Provincial authorities carried out the majority of the movement's tasks. Achievements during the strengthening period often transformed into foundations for personal power. For example, during the Sino-Japanese War, one provincial fleet decided to fight while another would not. Such conflicts and regional differences did not allow for a successful completion of the movement.

(2) *Limited vision:* The Self-Strengtheners such as Li Hongzhang and Zeng Guofan did not intend to remake China into a modern state. All emphasis was placed on strengthening the existing order rather than replacing it. Thus, outdated and crooked order prevailed, while the military received the bulk of the combined effort at strengthening.

(3) *Shortage of capital:* The initiation and growth of industries and enterprises were restricted. Since profits were often distributed among shareholders and not re-invested, capital formation became increasingly difficult.

(4) *Foreign imperialism:* The government's attention was divided between internal and external enemies. The cost of China's defense against the invasion of foreigners was enormous. Thus, the government incurred vast military expenditures and indemnities.

(5) *Technical backwardness and moral degradation:* The main issue surrounded the taboo that was placed upon foreign issues, which chased away men of talent and integrity who could have otherwise contributed to the leadership of the country. This resulted in an overabundance of incompetence and frequent cases of corruption in the Self-Strengthening Movement.

(6) *Social and Psychological Inertia:* The great majority of the scholar-official class regarded foreign affairs and Western-style enterprises as "dirty" and "vulgar." This commenced a movement towards anti-foreign material and ideas, thus strengthening China's age-old belief that it was the center of the world.

Despite the Self-Strengthening Movement's shortcomings, it managed to sow the seeds of modern capitalism in China. It also contributed to the development of great metropolises such as Shanghai, Nanjing, Tianjin, Fuzhou, Guangzhou, and Hankou.

Imperial Palace, Beijing

CHAPTER 5

ATTACK ON CHINA'S FRONTIERS BY JAPAN

During the last three decades of the 19th century, imperialism was on the rise in China. Imperial empires such as Britain, France, Russia and Japan encroached upon China's territory beginning with its frontier areas and tributary states, and then moving inward. This resulted in the virtual partition of China by the end of the 19th century.

5.1 THE TAIWAN CRISIS AND THE LIUQIU DISPUTE

Off the southern coast of the nation of Japan lay a multitude of small, inhabited islands termed the Liuqiu (or *Ryukyu* in Japanese). For a number of centuries, this group of islands had been paying tribute to China and showing its subordination to the Middle Kingdom. However, upon the arrival of the early 17th century, the Satsuma feudal domain of Tokugawa Japan began to extend its power and seize control over the islands. This seizure, more specifically, began in the year 1609. The interest on the part of Satsuma was specifically directed over the region for trade purposes. As a result, the Liuqiuan people began to pay tribute to Japan's powerful domain, in addition to China. Thus, as Japanese interest in the complete seizure of the Liuqiu Islands increased, so did Chinese apprehension towards the potential danger of the small band of islands.

It was not until 1871 that the Japanese began to exhibit offensive efforts towards the potential overtaking of these islands. This "military action" was the result of their efforts to assist with the retrieval of several Liuqiuan citizens. During 1871, a destructive typhoon caused two Liuqiuan ships to be overturned, and ultimately 66 individuals were eventually shipwrecked and recovered off the coast of Taiwan. At the time, half of the population of Taiwan was termed "civilized." The remaining half was considered to be barbaric aborigine. These aborigines murdered 54 of the stranded individuals. The remaining 12 were saved by the Chinese and sent back to Liuqiu. This action by the Taiwan aborigines did not amuse the Tokyo government at the time.

Two years later, in 1873, a group of Japanese shipwreck survivors were also maltreated by the aborigines in Taiwan. As a result, Japan decided to send a military expedition of thirty-six hundred men to Taiwan to punish the murderers. However, upon arriving in Taiwan, the Japanese soldiers were unequipped to handle the mountainous environment, and some were ultimately killed by the native aborigines. The losses incurred by the Japanese were settled and repaid in 1874, by the Chinese government under the Sino-Japanese Convention. The terms of the treaty stated that the actions demonstrated by the Japanese could not be deemed inappropriate. Therefore, the Japanese government and military should be repaid and compensated for the losses incurred during the shipwreck and the eventual murder of Japanese soldiers in Taiwan. Immediately following the inauguration of the treaty, an abundance of French legal administrators were consulted in order to interpret the treaty. Because of the ambiguity of the treaty and the foundation of International Law, it was determined that compensation should be provided for both the Liuqiuan people and the Japanese shipwreck incidents. This was one step in the Japanese advancement towards the complete acquisition of Liuqiu. The next step involved the actual method of seizing the islands for their own purposes.

The Japanese followed three steps in annexing the kingdom of Liuqiu. First, it was proposed that the kingdom cease relations and tributes that were sent to China immediately. Second, the king of Liuqiu must leave the country and take up permanent residence in Japan. This would leave no independent ruling power in the islands. Finally, several government-related Japanese officials would be sent to Liuqiu, to establish a sovereign Japanese branch of power. The Chinese, due to the fact that they did not have any concrete naval force, did not challenge this plan. The reality that the Beijing government was about to engage in a border war with Russia did not allow the nation to engage in a war on two fronts. In April 1879, the complete annexation of Liuqiu took place, leaving the island nation defenseless. The Liuqiu Islands were no longer an independent region. They were the property of Japan, becoming its Okinawa Prefecture.

The response of the Chinese resembled that of a helpless nation seeking the aid of others. They initially looked to a powerful nation located to the east of them, the United States, particularly through the good offices of former President Ulysses S. Grant. However, to their dismay, the only advice they received was to settle their quarrel with Japan through

33

peaceful measures — in other words, to discuss a diplomatic settlement. During the negotiations of 1879 through 1881, both nations discussed an alternative division of the Liuqiu Islands. China, however, refused any unreasonable and unfair settlement, and as a result no agreement was reached regarding the future of the Liuqiu Kingdom. With the "success" of the annexation of Liuqiu, the Japanese leaders continued on with their hunger for expansion. They looked next to the north — more specifically, to Korea.

5.2   JAPAN'S ENCROACHMENT INTO KOREA

For a period of time, interest in the diminutive nation of Korea constantly seemed to be on the minds on the Japanese ruling party. Upon gaining control of Liuqiu, the nation of Japan began to look in other directions for the opportunity to expand its national power. The nation of Korea was one of the feasible options. Rather than a complete and thorough militaristic takeover of the nation, the Tokyo government was determined to use a more intellectual and moderate tactic to open Korea peacefully. In the year 1875, Japanese warships were stationed and surveyed the coast of Korea. The Korean military took the initiative to fire upon the single ship. To resolve this situation, which had the potential to lead to dramatic consequences for Korea more so than for Japan, the Treaty of Kanghwa was signed on February 27, 1876. This treaty, which intended on improving diplomatic relations between both nations, improved economic opportunities for the Japanese by opening up the Korean ports of Inchon and Wonsan for trade, in addition to the existing port, Pusan. The Chinese rapidly became alarmed; for centuries the Koreans had been paying tribute to them, and now, Japanese interests and potential control over the nation increased tenfold, almost overnight with these new financial options.

While conflict among external nations existed, another struggle was taking place inside Korea that was shaping the political life of this nation. The governmental class was divided based on its ideas about reform: Conservatives vs. Progressives. The Progressives held the opinion that change was inevitable and was in the best interest of the nation. At the time, this viewpoint resembled Japanese ideals for modernization. This party, led by Yi Ha-ung, or Taewongun (meaning "Grand Prince), desired change in Korea's three systems: land tax, relief grain, and military service. The conservatives had views that adhered to the existing way of ruling. Essentially they desired governmental action and political decisions to remain as they were. As a result, both the Chinese and Japanese began to take notice, especially of the Taewongun who, in 1822, aided in the promotion of an anti-foreign uprising. This insurrection resulted in an attack on a Japanese delegation stationed in the country. Both the Chinese and Japanese sent troops to help their respective allies. The Chinese still held the notion that "Korea was dependent on them due to the payment of tribute." Ultimately, as a direct result of the larger Chinese forces, they were able to hold down the Japanese resistance and remove the Taewongun from power.

The Chinese placed in power the Min ruling faction that adhered to a conservative reform policy. It was against any Japanese-style modernization. These beliefs angered those Koreans who were in favor of modernization, and as a result an insurrection was attempted by forces seeking to overthrow the government. The Korean forces were successful in assassinating several conservative ministers, but were eventually defeated by a Chinese force led by Yuan Shikai. This tension between Japan and China was halted, briefly, when a treaty was signed — the Li-Ito Convention in 1884. Li Hongzhang, who represented China, and Ito Hirobumi, who represented Japan, signed the treaty. The main provision of the treaty was that if either nation were to increase its respective military forces in Korea, it had to inform the other nation.

While Japanese and Chinese hostilities grew, the people of Korea were becoming discontent. Prior to 1860, Chinese religious influences were seen heavily in Korean culture. Chinese writings from the Jesuits at Beijing became known as "Western Learning," and concurrently were appearing in the Korean way of life. Those individuals who held ideals that differed began a religious cult known as the Tonghak, meaning "Eastern Learning." A man named Ch'oe Che-u led this movement. Ch'oe had a desire to create a world that would overcome that of the West through its magic, and supersede the existing Korean ideologies, such as Confucianism and Buddhism. In 1884, many followers of the Tonghak rose up and rebelled against the Korean ruling party, demanding reform. The Korean government was unable to suppress this hostile band of individuals, and pleaded with the Chinese for assistance. As Chinese forces began to accumulate, so did the Japanese military. However, before the Japanese soldiers arrived, the rebellion led by Tonghak followers was suppressed by a Chinese offensive. Thereafter, eight thousand Japanese soldiers arrived in Korea. When the Japanese refused to withdraw their troops and return home, the Chinese and the Korean government became discontent. What came next was a skirmish entitled the Sino-Japanese War.

5.3　THE SINO-JAPANESE WAR (1894-1895) AND CHINESE DEFEAT

Overall, the hostilities that existed between China and Japan were continually increasing. Korea may have been a factor in this tension that was inevitably going to lead both nations to war. Japanese interest in Korea was growing on a daily basis for economic, financial, and militaristic purposes. This

36

was alarming to the Chinese, due to their tributary relations with Korea. Even though Korea was termed "independent" and therefore was not under the sovereignty of exterior nations, the Chinese felt that Korea was dependent on them to some degree. The Tonghak Insurrection was essentially the final event that officially brought both nations to war. On August 1, 1894, a formal declaration of war was proclaimed, which marked the beginning of the Sino-Japanese War.

Initially, most in the West felt that China would be victorious in the war due to its overwhelming size. However, to Chinese dismay, the Japanese came out of the incursion victorious, partly due to their efficient modernization efforts. Japan's army seized control of Korean lands, and then proceeded to invade the Manchurian region. Their mode for success did not come on land, but rather by sea. On September 17, the Japanese fleet took complete control of the Yalu River. The capture of Port Arthur naval base in Southern Manchuria, and Weihaiwei on the coast of Shandong followed thereafter. As a direct consequence of their inability to provide any sort of defense, the Chinese had to proclaim their defeat and put forth a suggestion to stop the battle. On April 17, 1895, the Treaty of Shimonoseki was signed and essentially marked the end of Chinese dominance in the region.

For the longest time, the Chinese nation was known simply as the "Middle Kingdom." It was the dominant power over continental Asia. The Treaty of Shimonoseki established Japan, not China, as the most dominant nation. The individuals who signed the treaty were Li Hongzhang and Ito Hirobumi. The intricate stipulations of the treaty severely weakened Chinese power, both from an economic and military standpoint: (1) China had to relinquish Taiwan, the Pescadores Islands, and the Liaodong peninsula; (2) the independence of Korea had to be recognized and acknowledged by China; (3) a sum total of 200 million taels had to be paid by the Chinese as an indemnity; (4) more Chinese ports had to be opened for trade; and (5) a commercial treaty had to be formally negotiated and signed for economic purposes. This treaty was signed in the year 1895, which gave Japan an abundance of industrial and manufacturing luxuries that it did not have in the past. As if the losses suffered by China in the war and subsequent treaties were not enough, the Russians, Germans, and French further divided Chinese territory for their individual people. Inevitably, the amount that China lost — economically, financially, and militarily — was vast.

CHAPTER 6

IMPERIAL CHINA'S LAST STRUGGLES

6.1 THE HUNDRED DAY REFORM (1898)

The reform movement in China had been gathering momentum for ten years. Scholars, officials, and even the emperor and empress dowager recognized the need for extensive reform. However, each party differed on the question of the reform's nature, scope, and leadership. The reform movement in 1898 brought forth various new leaders, including Zhang Zhidong, the governor general at Wuhan; Weng Tonghe, an influential imperial tutor and president of the Board of Revenue; and Kang Youwei, a well-known radical thinker and idealist, who was accompanied by his disciple Liang Qichao. Both Zhang and Weng advocated a conservative reform based on a limited administrative reorganization, along with the adoption of Western methods to supplement the basic Chinese structure. Kang and Liang advocated a drastic institutional change, very similar to the patterns of change initiated by Peter the Great of Russia and Emperor Meiji of Japan. Emperor Guangxu (r.1875-1908) was won over by the persuasive Kang; however, Empress Dowager Cixi fervently opposed his ideas. At the age of forty, Kang had become the leader of a radical reform movement.

Kang's basic view on reform was that times had changed, and internal security was no longer China's priority. According to Kang, the government needed to consider the new problem of foreign relations and industrialization, and modernize its structure accordingly. Kang believed that the emperor's power must be wrested from the dowager. He formally submitted a proposal to the court that included the following main points: (1) a revision of the examination system and legal code; (2) the establishment of a governmental institution bureau and the creation of twelve new bureaus; (3) the establishment of bureaus of people's affairs in local self-government; (4) the creation of a Parliament in Beijing; (5) the establishment of a national assembly; and (6) the adoption of a constitution and the principle of division of power between the executive, legislative, and judicial branches. These main ideas combined would result in a constitutional monarchy to replace the age-old "imperial Confucian" system.

The Grand Council comprised four of Kang's assistants. The assistants became the de facto executives of reform. On September 12, 1898, the Grand Council issued an edict that declared that the basic principles of government were the same in China as in the West, and the reform movement would be used to place into effect those methods and principles that had proven sound, valid, and useful in the West. For one hundred and three days, from June 11 until September 20, some forty to fifty reform decrees were issued in rapid succession in the areas of education, government, industry, and international cultural exchange. These included: (1) Education: The establishment of an Imperial University at Beijing, modern schools to teach Chinese and Western studies, a medical school under the Imperial University, the publication of an official newspaper, and the opening of an exam in political economy; (2) Political Administration: The abolition of sinecure and unnecessary offices, the appointment of progressives in government, the development of new simplified administrative procedures, the encouragement of suggestions from citizens, and permission for Manchus to engage in trade; (3) Industry: The construction of a railway, encouragement of commercial development and entrepreneurial activity, and the beautification of the capital; (4) Other: The visitation of high officials to foreign countries, the protection of missionaries, preparation of a budget, and the simplification of legal codes. Unfortunately, the reform program was boycotted by high officials who either ignored or delayed the orders for reform. Many Chinese knew that the real power of the state was in the hands of the Empress Dowager, who opposed the reform altogether and subsequently killed the Hundred Day Reform by arresting the reformers and putting the emperor under "house arrest."

6.2   THE BOXER UPRISING (1900)

After the failure of the Hundred Day Reform, strong anti-foreign sentiments permeated not only the court under the Empress Dowager, but also spread amongst the scholars, officials, gentry, and the people at large. There was a growing sense of injustice that generated a desire for revenge due to years of foreign humiliation and war. The Chinese people, particularly a group known as the Boxers, felt antipathy toward Christianity and its disruption of the Chinese way of life, anger over imperial expansion, and fury over the influx of foreign imports, and the depressing effect it had on the national economy. *Boxer* was the name given by foreigners to a Chinese secret society called *Yi-he-quan*, translated as the "Righteous and

Harmonious Fists." Fundamental to the Boxer's program, and of primary appeal to the superstitious populace, was the practice of magic arts.

Originally an anti-Qing society, the Boxers became pro-dynastic and xenophobic in the 1890s. During this time, they were particularly active under the name of the Big Sword Society, in which they received secret encouragement from government officials in Shandong. Although foreigners began to protest governmental support of the organization, it continued to expand. With governmental support, the Boxers became more daring and dangerous, and subsequently began to burn railways and telegraph lines to symbolize their feelings of foreign enslavement. On June 3, 1900, the Boxers cut the railway between Beijing and Tianjin, and embarked on a rampage through northern China. On June 10, they burned the British summer legation in the West Hills, and a day later killed Sugiyama, the chancellor of the Japanese legation. Beijing and Tianjin were soon swarmed with Boxers who burned churches and foreign residences, killed Chinese converts and the German minister Clemens von Ketteler, and attacked the legation guards. The court was encouraged by the Boxers' success thus far, and declared war on the foreign powers on June 21.

Upon the Boxer invasion of the capital, the allied forces began to fight back, and the court subsequently fled the city. On October 23, the court re-established itself in Xi'an, but the allied forces had managed to still the Boxer rebellion. At this point in the rebellion, over 231 foreigners had been killed, as well as numerous Chinese Christians. Since the dowager refused to return to Beijing on the grounds that she feared untoward treatment and unacceptable terms being imposed on her, peace negotiations were drawn out in her absence. On December 24, 1900, the allies agreed on a joint note of twelve articles, which was later formalized into the Boxer Protocol.

The protocol contained three main objectives: (1) punishment of the guilty; (2) payment of an indemnity; and (3) various stipulations including apologies and the stationing of foreign troops in China. The court returned to Beijing on January 7, 1902.

6.3 ATTEMPT ON CONSTITUTIONALISM

On August 20, 1900, the dowager issued a decree that blamed herself for China's misfortune; she did this in an attempt to win foreign esteem and domestic respect. She then proclaimed the desire to institute a reform of her own: The Qing Reform of 1901-1905. The program was a shrewd effort on the part of the dowager to disguise her shame over her role in the Boxer Rebellion. Her insincerity was reflected by the fact that while she openly asked for suggestions from officials in the central and provincial governments, she secretly expressed her profound distaste for foreigners. Her reform program was essentially a failure; however, three improvements were actually attained: (1) the abolition of the civil service examinations; (2) the establishment of modern schools; and (3) the encouragement of students to study abroad.

The failure of the Qing reform coincided with Japan's victory over Russia in 1905. This victory proved to the Chinese that constitutionalism was effective, and the idea of such a government rapidly spread among governors-general and governors. The voice of constitutionalism was eventually taken over by Liang Qichao, who had lived in Japan during the Boxer years and acquired Western ideas. He expounded upon the ideas of liberty and equality in his journals, *Public Opinion, 1898-1902*, and *The New People's Miscellany, 1902-1907*. Liang believed that China was not ready for a truly democratic and representative government, but considered a constitutional monarchy more of an immediate and attainable goal.

While constitutionalism was a popular concept, it also faced much opposition. The radicals under Dr. Sun Yatsen counterattacked Liang's ideas with the ideas of a republic. The Empress Dowager considered constitutionalism the lesser of two evils and thus lent her support. On December 11, 1905, a delegation was sent to the U.S., Germany, Austria, Italy, Britain, France, and Belgium to investigate the prospect of constitutionalism in China. The delegation determined that Japan's constitution was most suitable to China, considering the geographical and cultural proximity between the two nations. Thus, the dowager approved a recommendation for a constitution on September 1, 1906. However, on November 7, 1906, the court issued a decree on the reform, stating that the goal would be to attain a form of modern constitutionalism that had an essence of old governmental procedures. In August of 1907, a Bureau of Constitutional Compilation was established, and a month later an official was dispatched to Japan to study constitutionalism. The government's wish to keep the process of constitutionalism rather slow led to the establishment of many different Constitution Protection clubs. The clubs encouraged many of their members to go to Beijing to petition for the early promulgation of the constitution. Under pressure, the court issued an "Outline of Constitution" and a parliamentary law, and prescribed a nine-year tutelage period before the constitution became effective. The outline gave the throne even greater power than that of the Japanese model.

The Empress Dowager had purposely constructed the nine-year tutelage period clause so that she would not be alive when the constitution was installed. Unfortunately, she did not foresee that her death would come only months after the court issued the "Outline of Constitution." Furthermore, the day before the dowager's death — November 14, 1908 — the emperor Guangxu suspiciously died as well, gracing the three-year-old Puyi with the title of emperor and the second Prince

Chun as regent. On February 17, 1909, Prince Chun attempted to continue the reforms with the establishment of provincial assemblies. In addition, he announced that he would shorten the period of constitutional prep from nine to six years. He then organized a Royal Cabinet on May 8, 1911, with eleven appointees, eight of whom were Manchus. The Manchu dominance convinced the Chinese that genuine constitutionalism was impossible under the Manchu leadership. Disillusion and disappointment, combined with mounting anti-Manchu sentiment, began to sway public feeling toward the revolutionary cause.

Pool at Chin Temple, Taiyuan

CHAPTER 7

THE REVOLUTION FOR DEMOCRACY

7.1   DR. SUN YATSEN, THE REVOLUTIONARY LEADER

Dr. Sun Yatsen, also known as the Father of the Chinese Revolution, was born on November 12, 1866, in Xiangshan, Guangdong, as the second son of peasant parents. As many Chinese southerners often did during that time, Sun's parents sought their family's livelihood abroad by sending their oldest son off to Hawaii to work. In 1879, at the tender age of 13, Sun was also sent to Hawaii, but with the intention of his going to school. Congruent with his Western education, Sun became involved with Christianity, and for fear of a formal baptism taking place, Sun's older brother sent him back to China. Back in China, Sun's Western influences surfaced as he witnessed China's defeat by France in 1885, and began to develop ideas about overthrowing the dynasty. Conditions in

China began to rapidly deteriorate, and Sun embarked on a path as a reformer.

At the age of 20, Sun enrolled in the Baoji Medical School at Guangzhou, but later transferred to the College of Medicine for Chinese in Hong Kong, since the British colony afforded more freedom and revolutionary activity. Sun graduated first in his class, and began a practice in Macao in 1892. Henceforth, he was known as Dr. Sun, and he still maintained his reformist position. However, the Chinese government ignored him since he was not educated in mainland China. As a means to establish contacts and build his own reputation, Dr. Sun worked for free throughout Guangzhou. An old friend and schoolmate, Zheng Shiliang, also fostered contacts for Sun through his wide connections with secret societies. The turning point in Dr. Sun's political career came in the summer of 1894, when Sun and his friend, Lu Haodong, went north to see the state of affairs in the capital. Sun was disgusted at what he saw, determining that reform was not the answer. In the fall of 1894, Dr. Sun went to Honolulu to seek aid from Chinese residing overseas, requesting help from members of secret societies, Christian converts, and missionaries. As a result, he was able to establish the Revive China Society on November 24. Henceforth, Dr. Sun became a revolutionary leader.

From the establishment of the overseas Revive China Society throughout 1896, Sun's movement gained momentum, and his influence expanded. On October 26, 1895, Dr. Sun established his connection with a local militia, and scheduled an uprising in Guangzhou. Unfortunately, the plot was discovered and Dr. Sun was forced to flee China; initially he sought refuge in Hong Kong, but when he learned he had been banned for five years, he fled to Japan. While in Japan, Sun established another Revive China Society branch, and gained the support of many Japanese sympathizers. With confidence, he moved on to Honolulu to promote the revolution, only to find that many of his previous supporters had grown indifferent after the abortive Guangzhou uprising. Dr. Sun then decided to go to London in October of 1896 to develop his revolutionary plan, but the agents of the Chinese embassy captured him on October 11. This incident became known as the "London Kidnap." Sun was eventually released, and the incident received much publicity. As a result, he was transformed into a celebrity overnight. The event dramatically helped Dr. Sun's revolutionary cause.

7.2   THE THREE PEOPLE'S PRINCIPLES AND REVOLUTIONARY STRUGGLES

After being released from the Chinese embassy in London, Dr. Sun stayed in England for nine months and developed his famous *Three People's Principles*. The principles include People's National Consciousness (Nationalism), People's Rights (Democracy), and People's Livelihood (Socialism), all of which became the revolutionary philosophy of Dr. Sun and his followers. In fact, the Three People's Principles are still the abiding creed of the government in Taiwan today. The principle of Nationalism, or People's National Consciousness, called for the overthrow of the alien Manchu rule and removal of foreign imperialist control. The second principle, democracy, or People's Rights, called for the achievement of (1) four rights: initiative, referendum, election, and recall; and (2) five powers for the government: executive, legislative, judicial, control, and examination. The last principle, People's Livelihood, or Socialism, stressed the need for regulating capital and equalizing the land. It was based on an ancient Chinese utopian idea of "land to the tiller."

Back in Japan, by 1897 Dr. Sun was considered the man destined to regenerate China for the cause of Pan-Asianism. In

China, however, many citizens were very reluctant to join the movement for fear of retaliation by the Manchu government. Dr. Sun took advantage of the Boxer Rebellion in 1900, and organized another uprising with two fronts: one at Weizhou and the other in Guangzhou. Once again, Sun's plot was discovered, and although he did not participate in the uprisings himself, he was forced to flee to Japanese-occupied Taiwan. With a change of government in Japan, all previous assistance that Sun had been receiving was cancelled, and Sun was then not even permitted to leave the island. The Qing court's mismanagement of the Boxer Rebellion led many people to look upon Sun with favor, and soon revolutionary publications were popping up in both China and Japan. Contributors to the publications were mostly intellectuals and members of secret societies, as opposed to the general public. Some of the publications were entitled *The Revolutionary Army* and *Twentieth Century China*, while secret societies emerged under the names of the Recovery Society, China Revival Society, and the Gelao Brotherhood Association.

From 1902 to 1905, Dr. Sun traveled widely in order to promote his revolution and seek international support. He set up revolutionary groups throughout the world, with the largest located in Tokyo, thus sowing the seeds of a new revolutionary party. Dr. Sun decided to unify all the revolutionary groups to avoid any duplication of efforts, and he thus created the Chinese United League (Tongmeng hui) on August 20, 1905. This league, with Dr. Sun as chairman, became his major revolutionary organization. Although membership in the league was only 70 upon its inauguration, within a year the membership grew to 963 people. Through this organization, the younger generations in China began to turn to the revolutionary side, which fundamentally changed the character and style of the revolution. Dr. Sun moved to the mainstream of Chinese nationalism, and the Chinese United League became known as the "Mother of the Chinese Revolution."

The period that followed the creation of the Chinese United League, during the years 1905-1911, saw one uprising after another. One might deem this successful, in terms of the actual occurrence of the uprising; however, not much occurred in the way of overthrowing the decaying Manchu rule. During these rebellions, Dr. Sun was overseas perfecting his revolutionary plan. Most of the rebellions took place in the south and southwest, where proximity to Hong Kong and Hanoi provided greater freedom for plotting and organizing the events. In April 1911, there was an attempt to capture the provincial capital of Guangzhou. This attempt, although not completely successful, managed to stir up the public enough that it foreshadowed the success of the next attempt at Wuchang half a year later. The government's decision to nationalize the railways further infuriated the people, and led to the Wuchang revolution.[1]

To control the unrest in Sichuan spawned by the railway controversy, the Qing government transferred part of the Hubei New Army there. On October 9, 1911, a bomb accidentally exploded in the revolutionary headquarters, and during the police raid in the building, the traitors of the New Army were discovered. With nothing to lose (since the Qing already knew of their treason), the New Army members decided to strike,

---

[1] In 1905, the provincial governments of Guangdong, Hunan, and Hubei bought the rights to construct the parts of the railway that ran through their respective provinces; however, before construction was complete, they ran out of resources. The Qing government decided that, through the help of foreign loans, it would nationalize the railroad, thereby paying an indemnity to those who had invested in the railways. However, the sense of injustice was so powerful that popular uprisings were all but inevitable, particularly in Sichuan. The railway controversy and the revolution had fused into one issue.

affording the engineering unit an opportunity to seize the government munitions depot in Wuchang. The governor-general and military commander both fled, and by noon of October 10 the rebels had complete control of the city. Other provinces began to follow suit and within a month and a half, 15 provinces had seceded from the Qing dynasty. By December 1911, both Shanghai and Nanjing had been placed under revolutionary control, and a provincial government was established, in preparation for Dr. Sun's return from abroad for leadership.

7.3 BIRTH OF THE REPUBLIC OF CHINA (1912)

Upon learning of the Wuchang Revolution, Dr. Sun left Denver, Colorado for London to gain British support. He had hoped that by gaining diplomatic recognition for the new government he could stop the previous loan negotiations with the Qing government, and prevent Japan from aiding the fallen Manchus. After London, Sun traveled on to France for the same purposes, and returned to Shanghai by the end of December. On December 25, Dr. Sun was elected the provisional president of the Republic of China. The first day of the republic was designated January 1, 1912; however, the Manchu abdication of the throne was yet to come.

The series of uprisings and seizures of major cities led the Manchu rulers to seek help from the powerful military leader, Yuan Shikai. After Yuan delivered a shattering blow to the revolutionary forces, a British minister — John Jordan — was persuaded to negotiate a truce between the two sides. On December 1, it was agreed that if Yuan would support the republic and force the abdication of the Qing court, then the presidency of the new republic would be his. When Sun was elected president of the republic anyway on December 25, Yuan was furious and broke off the peace negotiations. The revolutionaries, including Dr. Sun, soon realized that the revolution could not survive without Yuan on their side. Sun was willing to step down from the presidency since his first priority had been to overthrow the Manchus and establish a republic. At this point, Sun was also irritated with his followers, who seemed to be ignoring the Three People's Principles.

During January 17-19, 1912, there were three imperial conferences held to deliberate the possible abdication of the throne. It was not until February 1, 1912, however, that the dowager announced the formal abdication to Yuan. On February 12, Yuan read a prepared imperial "script" announcing the abdication, thus ending the 268-year Qing rule and the last of China's dynasties. Within the formal abdication "script," Yuan inserted his own provision, which authorized him to organize a provisional republican government and negotiate national reunification. The purpose of this insertion was to show that he derived his power from both the revolutionary government in Nanjing (i.e. Dr. Sun) and also the Qing emperor. On February 13, 1912, Parliament formally elected Yuan as president of the Republic of China, and he was inaugurated in Beijing on March 10. The United States was the first to diplomatically recognize the new republic, but unfortunately the Republic of China was only a republic in name, not in reality. With Yuan Shikai in charge, the road was paved for warlordism and attempts to revive the imperial system.

Top of Great Wall, Badalin

CHAPTER 8

FAILURE OF THE EARLY REPUBLIC

8.1   YUAN SHIKAI, THE PRESIDENT

After the Qing dynasty's abdication of the throne on February 12, 1912, and Dr. Sun Yatsen's resignation from the presidency the following day, Yuan Shikai became the president of the new Republic of China. Being a man with no principles, Yuan disrupted the plans of the revolutionaries in order to pursue his own interests.

To consolidate his power, Yuan refused to move the capital from Beijing (his power base) to Nanjing, where the revolutionaries' power was strong. Then, in the first cabinet, he appointed his military followers to take charge of the four important ministries: Foreign Affairs, Interior Affairs, War, and Navy, and left the other four less important ones to the revolutionary leaders. Soon after, Yuan successfully reduced the power of the cabinet and the revolutionaries. He refused to pay wages to the 50,000 troops of Huang Xing, who was the preferred choice of the revolutionaries to be Minister of War, in order to disband them and to diminish Huang's power. In addition, Yuan humiliatingly compelled Premier Tang Shaoyi to resign from his post of resident-general of Nanjing. Tang left and was followed by the four cabinet ministers from the revolutionary camp. Under Yuan, the cabinet was a tool of the president.

The Nationalist Party (Guomindang) was founded in December 1912 under the effective guidance of Song Jiaoren, one of Dr. Sun's associates; it was a conglomeration of five political parties, including the Chinese United League. Song not only got the support from Huang, but also respect from the constitutionalists. In the 1913 national election, Song strongly campaigned against Yuan's administration. His party got a majority of seats in the parliament. Song's leadership ability and his critique of presidential excesses seriously irritated Yuan. Failing to bribe him, Yuan conspired with Premier Zhao Bingjun, and had Song assassinated in March 1913. Yuan was blamed for the assassination of his political opponent.

A reorganization loan of £25 million, which Yuan sought from the Five Power Banking Consortium in April 1913, increased hatred for him among the Nationalists. When Dr. Sun and Huang opposed the new parliament, Duan Qirui, Yuan's acting premier, surrounded the parliament with troops. A permanent split between Yuan and the revolutionaries occured when Nationalist members of parliament tried to impeach the government. Yuan unexpectedly dismissed the Nationalist military governors of Jiangxi, Guangdong, and Anhui, and put his army on alert in the south.

8.2   DR. SUN YATSEN'S SECOND REVOLUTION

In the summer of 1913, seven southern provinces declared their independence by rebelling against Yuan and starting the so-called Second Revolution. This rebellion was suppressed within a few months. Dr. Sun and other instigators fled to Japan. Yuan's generals took over control of the Yangzi area and became provincial warlords.

Yuan was no longer satisfied with the power and title of president; he coveted the overarching power associated with being emperor. His ultimate goal contrasted with his pledge in 1912 to defend the republic and put the monarchy out of existence. Intimidating parliament into voting for him, Yuan was formally elected as president in October 1913. He dissolved the Nationalist Party on November 4, and withdrew the credentials of its 438 parliamentarians under the pretext of its association with the Second Revolution. On March 18, 1914, Yuan revised the constitution, creating a life-long presidency. A new Constitutional Compact, published on May 1, set the presidential term at 10 years. This term could be renewed by an indefinite number of re-elections; the Constitutional Compact also guaranteed the right of the president to choose his own successor.

To counteract the recent set of events, Dr. Sun reorganized the Nationalist Party, tightened its structure, and renamed it the Chinese Revolutionary Party on July 8, 1914. A Chinese Revolutionary Army was established to fight Yuan's abuse of the presidency and betrayal of the republic. Dr. Sun also launched a new political theory, the Three-stage Formula, to deal with the Yuan regime: First, a phase of military rule would be organized to develop revolutionary power; a tutelage stage would follow to ensure that the military leaders would instruct people in the ideas of constitutional rights; and finally

57

a constitutional phase would be established to set aside the military government and allow the people to elect their own constitutional government.

To materialize his monarchical dream, Yuan moved to gain foreign support and international recognition. Yuan accepted the infamous Twenty-One Demands from Japan, which could be grouped into five parts: (1) recognition of Japan's role in Shandong; (2) a special position for Japan in Manchuria and Inner Mongolia; (3) joint operation of China's iron and steel industries; (4) non-alienation of coastal areas to any third power; and (5) control over China's domestic administration. In addition, he signed agreements with Russia and Britain, permitting self-government for Outer Mongolia and Tibet, respectively.

Subsequently, Yuan launched the Peace-Planning Society on August 21, 1915, as a part of his domestic movement toward the emperorship. Behind the scenes, Yuan brought in famous scholars such as Yan Fu to write articles creating counterfeit public opinion that China was not ready for democracy and should switch back to the monarchical system. An article by Dr. Frank J. Goodnow, Yuan's American advisor on constitutional issues and the president of the Johns Hopkins University, doubted the fitness of a democracy and suggested the rightness of constitutional monarchy for China. The article was also used as an indication that Yuan had international support. Many petitions calling for a change in the governmental system were submitted to the National People's Representative Assembly, which approved the return of a monarchy on November 20, 1915. Yuan played a reluctant man, accepted the title, and decreed 1916 the start of his new reign called, ironically, the Glorious Constitution (Hongxian).

Widespread rebellions arose, and numerous provinces declared independence. In Yunnan, revolutionaries including Cai E and Liang Qichao, established a National Protection Army to fight Yuan and defend the republic. After Yuan refused a two-day ultimatum to cancel his monarchist movement, Yunnan declared independence on December 25, 1915. The National Protection Army set out on a multi-front campaign to attack Yuan's forces. Realizing he had made a big mistake, Yuan decided to postpone his enthronement, scheduled for January 1, 1916. Consequently, the Japanese government sent a notice stating the withdrawal of its support to Yuan. Yuan had to abandon his reign on March 22, 1916. Furthermore, the Military Affairs Council, which united the various revolutionary groups, and a group of well-known citizens from 19 provinces refused to recognize Yuan as president. Yuan was deserted by his henchmen. He died in disgrace on June 6, 1916, and with him the movement for monarchism in China.

8.3   RISE OF WARLORDISM: CHINA IN DISINTEGRATION

After Yuan died, the nation disintegrated into warlord groups and territories. The lack of a strong constitution led to the fight for the ultimate power of the presidency. The period of Warlordism (1916-1928) was indeed the darkest period in republican history.

Li Yuanhong took over the presidency on June 7, 1916. The question of the validity of different constitutions arose. There was conflict between the supporters of the southern revolutionaries who wanted to re-establish the legality of the 1912 constitution, and those of Premier Duan Qirui in Beijing who supported the 1914 constitution. The 1912 constitution was reinstated after the naval commander at Shanghai, Feng Guozhang, declared independence from the Beijing regime on

June 25 and gave his support to the south. After President Li agreed to reestablish the old parliament and reappoint Duan as Premier, the revolutionaries abolished the Military Affairs Council in favor of national unification.

Deserted by his henchmen during a clash with Premier Duan over a declaration of war with Germany, President Li Yuanhong desperately turned to Zhang Xun, the military governor in Anhui, for support. Zhang agreed to mediate the situation on the condition that Li dissolve the parliament. Li had no choice but to fulfill the request. Then, with the support of Kang Youwei, and a secret agreement with the Beiyang leaders Duan and Feng, Zhang restored the last Manchu emperor, Puyi, to the throne on July 1, 1917 and revived the Qing institutions, ranks, and positions as well. Zhang became the chief minister of the cabinet and the governor-general of Zhili, displacing Cao Kun. Duan was left out of the office allocation process regardless of his support. Hence, Cao and Duan gathered the Beiyang forces to drive Zhang and his 20,000 soldiers out of Beijing on July 12. This ended the restoration movement and began a period of civil war among the warlords.

Duan again became the premier. He got support from the so-called Research Clique under Liang Qichao to form a new republic. Once Duan organized a new provisional parliament on November 10, 1917, the southern revolutionaries accused him of violating the 1912 constitution. Once again Dr. Sun Yatsen established a military government in Guangzhou and initiated a Constitution Protection Movement.

After revision of the election and organization laws of the 1912 constitution, Duan organized a new alliance to rally his own supporters. The Anfu Club, named for the key provinces of Anhui and Fujian, won the majority of seats in the re-elected parliament on August 12, 1918, while the Research

Clique received approximately 30. Two days later, the Anfu Parliament passed a declaration of war against Germany, giving Duan an opportunity to negotiate the loans of 145 million *yen* from the Japanese. At the same time, Duan mobilized the troops to destroy the military government in Guangzhou.

President Feng Guozhang, successor to Li Yuanhong, nonetheless favored a peaceful resolution to the domestic conflicts. This disagreement split the Beiyang Group into the Anhui Clique under Duan and the Zhili Clique under Feng. Blocked by Feng's followers, Duan's campaign against the Constitution Protection Army failed. Duan finally resigned on November 22, 1918. The period of chaos and disorder ended with the victory of the Zhili group in support of the Manchuria Clique under Zhang Zuolin. However, in April 1922 another clash broke out between them. Once again, the Zhili group won. Zhang Zuolin declared the independence of Manchuria from the Beijing regime.

Even though there was strong opposition among some elements within the group, the Zhili Clique had hoped to achieve national unification through a peaceful settlement with the Guangzhou government, and therefore offered the presidency to Li Yuanhong. In mid-1922, a split between the Zhili warlords occurred. The Loyang faction under Wu Peifu sought the military conquest of China and supported President Li. The Tianjin-Baoding faction opposed Wu and supported Cao Kun for president. At last, President Li was driven out of office. Cao Kun became president through the bribery of some members of parliament in October 1923.

Sickened by the corruption, people put their hope in the revolutionary government in Guangzhou. But the Constitution Protection Movement had made little progress. Although Dr. Sun was made generalissimo, he was forced out of the military government in May 1917 by Lu Rongting of Guangdong and Guangxi, the real commander. Escaping to Shanghai, Dr. Sun engaged himself mainly in writing the "Outline of National Reconstruction" and planning party reorganization. On October 10, 1919, he reorganzied the Chinese Revolutionary Party and renamed it the Chinese Nationalist Party. In the end, he was able to reclaim Guangzhou and revive the military regime. In opposition to warlord control in Beijing, the formal establishment of a republican government took place on April 2, 1921, with Dr. Sun as president. On February 3, 1922, an unexpected uprising in Guangzhou led by a former supporter, Chen Jiongming, stopped Dr. Sun from starting his Northern Expedition.

After Cao Kun became president in October 1923, Feng Yuxiang moved his troops forward from Manchuria to Beijing. This second Zhili-Fengtian war brought about the collapse of the Zhili forces. With the support of his National People's Party, Feng reorganized the cabinet and drove President Cao Kun out of the capital on November 2, 1924. In an effort to attain national unification, the National People's Party, the Fengtian Clique, and the Anhui Clique mutually asked Duan Qirui to be the executive of a provisional government. Dr. Sun was invited to Beijing; however, he was in bad health and died on March 12, 1925. Dr. Sun did not live to see his dream of a unified China realized, thus he died a broken man. Yet his determination and dedication changed the face of Chinese history. As a result, Dr. Sun is also often said to be the Father of Modern China.

CHAPTER 9

THE INTELLECTUAL REVOLUTION

9.1   THE NEW CULTURE MOVEMENT

The New Culture Movement between 1915 and 1919 was the result of years of intellectual, political, social, and economic ferment. It was the climax of a mental awakening that had begun in 1915, or in those early years following the 1911 Revolution that had overthrown the Qing dynasty but failed to establish a new social order. It was also the start of a movement of growing political awareness. It enlightened young intellectuals and workers. This resulted in both the growth of modern nationalism and a cultural renaissance, which broadly focused on investigating and transforming the socially and intellectually repressive features of traditional culture among Chinese intellectuals.

It was a period of fermentation and transition, also producing strong counter-currents to the trends being received from the West. However, the prevailing trend was towards popular acceptance of such ideals as individualism, freedom, progress, democracy, and science among the intelligentsia. Chen Duxiu was one of the Chinese pioneers enlightened by Western culture; he was encouraged by Cai Yuanpei — the chancellor of Peking University at the time — whose thoughts represented an attempt to synthesize the Chinese classical tradition with the libertarianism of the Modern European West. The tenets of Chen Duxiu's early political philosophy reflected the ideas of the French Revolution; however, Chen's later ideas approached the concepts of Leninism.

This Communist trend, which mimicked that of the Russian Revolution, led to a fundamental split in Chinese political thought: Chen and Li Dazhao (the first Chinese convert to Communism) were the forerunners of the Communist school of thought in China, and Hu Shi was the leading advocate for Western democracy, the ideas of John Dewey, and pragmatism. Right before World War I, these intellectuals spearheaded a movement that reached out in many directions and touched many aspects of Chinese society. The movement may be roughly divided into several aspects, presented as: (1) the attack on Confucianism; (2) the proclamation of a new philosophy of life and "science"; (3) the Literary Revolution; and 4) the debate on Chinese and Western cultural values.

The New Culture Movement had a significant impact on China's modern development. It argued that feudal despotism had stifled the development of the scientific and rational spirit of the Chinese nation, and that it was responsible for both the persistence of superstition, a benighted sense of obedience, and ignorance. It was also blamed for the disastrous consequences of undeveloped Chinese science and technology and the backward nature of Chinese social life. A great number of Western philosophies had been introduced into China, some of which produced intense shock and profound influence in the literary sphere. They fastened an iconoclastic spirit and strove for individual freedom.

9.2   THE MAY FOURTH INCIDENT (1919)

On May 4, 1919, about 5,000 students in Beijing held a huge demonstration against the decision of the Versailles Peace Conference to accept Japanese control of the former German concessions in Shandong Province. It was at once an explosion of public anger, an outburst of nationalism, an expression of deep disappointment in the West, and a violent indictment of the "traitorous" warlord government in Beijing. Nationalism, public opinion, and mass demonstrations had emerged as new forces in Chinese politics. Some historians today hail the May Fourth incident as the first serious mass movement in Chinese history.

The May Fourth Movement, which began in Beijing and later spread to other cities throughout China, incorporated the broader themes of the New Culture Movement. It has become one of the most important movements in Chinese history. Near the end of April 1919, Chinese student organizations, upon hearing rumors about China's failure in the Paris Conference, agreed to hold mass demonstrations in Beijing on May 7 — this was National Humiliation Day, the fourth anniversary of Japan's ultimatum of the Twenty-One Demands. However, the date was moved to May 4 in order to avoid a conflict with another planned rally in Beijing. The demonstration did not remain peaceful. On the afternoon of May 4, over 3,000 students from thirteen colleges and universities in Beijing met in Tiananmen to call for the Chinese to stand up and oppose foreign domination, especially Japanese occupation of Qingdao (capital of Shandong Province). They pledged an oath stating: (1) China's territory may be conquered, but it cannot be given away; and (2) the Chinese people may be massacred, but they will not surrender. Following the meeting in Tiananmen, the students began an orderly march East towards Chongwenmen. The students carried banners written in Chinese, English, and French. After marching past Chongwenmen, the students headed for the Diplomatic Quarter but were turned away by the police.

The students then headed to the home of Cao Rulin, the foreign minister who had negotiated the Twenty-One Demands in 1915 and was now urging Chinese ratification of the Treaty of Versailles. By the time students reached his house, he had already slipped away. Members of his family were beaten and his house was set on fire. The students, with the help of their teachers, organized an immediate strike and further demonstrations. Demonstrations spread rapidly throughout major cities in China. In some areas, the demonstrations were quickly suppressed. As demonstrations continued in Beijing, arrests increased. When the Beijing jails were full, the authorities converted university buildings into jails.

At the beginning, most demonstrators were young men. This situation changed as time went on. In Tianjin, female students organized an Association of Women Comrades, and in Beijing more than 1,000 female students protested in front of the President's house on June 4 and 5. The student strike also spread to other cities and it was joined by shopkeepers, industrial workers, and employees in commercial establishments all over China. People stopped buying Japanese goods. The protesters achieved great success. Cao Rulin was forced to resign, and on June 28 there were no Chinese representatives present at the signing of the Treaty of Versailles. The May Fourth Movement continued on into the 1920s under the broader title of the New Culture Movement.

For contemporary Chinese historians, May Fourth is an important date. They regard it as the turning point between the modern and contemporary history of their country. For the first time, the May Fourth Movement had united the defense of national sovereignty with the struggle against "feudal" rule, thus opening a new chapter in China's revolutionary experience. It also started a whole series of new processes, which were to prove decisive for the course of Chinese history up to and even beyond 1949 after the Communists took power.

9.3 FOUNDING OF THE CHINESE COMMUNIST PARTY (1921)

Another important consequence of the May Fourth Movement was the introduction of Communism into China and the birth of the Chinese Communist Party. Disappointed by the betrayal of the Western countries in Versailles and encouraged by the success of the Russian revolution, some Chinese turned to Communism, which provided China with another solution. The Chinese Communist Party was founded in 1921, two years after the May Fourth Incident.

Communism was introduced to the Chinese around 1905, when the republican newspaper, *Min Bao,* published a biography of Karl Marx. After that, articles on Communism were introduced to Chinese intellectuals by various paths. The intellectual and psychological appeal of Marxism was further strengthened and encouraged by the Leninist theory of imperialism. Li Dazhao, the chief librarian of Peking University and one of the first converts to Marxism, founded the New Tide Society (*Xin Chao She*) in 1918 and commented on "The Victory of Bolshevism." He also edited a whole issue on Marxism in the journal *New Youth* in 1919. His students, as well as his library assistant, Mao Zedong, were all attracted to this idea as a new solution to save China from the imperialist countries' invasion. In the same year, they formed the Marxist Research Society, which was replaced by the Society for the Study of Socialism at the end of 1919. By March 1920, the various Marxist groups in Beijing had united to form the Beijing Society for the Study of Marxist Theory.

The second Chinese intellectual who was converted to Communism was Chen Duxiu. After being forced to resign from Peking University due to his participation in the May Fourth Movement, he gave up his faith in Western democracy and was converted to Marxism in Shanghai, where he organized a Marxist Study Society and a Socialist Youth Corps in 1920. These organizations were considered the forerunners of the Chinese Communist Party.

Meanwhile, Grigorii Boitinsky, an agent of the Comintern (Communist International), conferred with both Li Dazhao and Chen Duxiu about organizing a political party. After the conferences, party branches in Shanghai and Beijing came into being.

The First National Congress of the Chinese Communist Party was secretly held at a girls' boarding school in the French concession of Shanghai on July 23, 1921, which proclaimed the founding of the Party. Twelve delegates representing 57 members attended the meeting. However, Chen Duxiu and Li Dazhao were both absent. They were honored as the co-founders of the CCP. Although the central party headquarters was set up in Shanghai, the Marxist study group headed by Li Dazhao in Beijing stayed virtually independent. The situation of "Chen in the south, Li in the north" (*nan Chen bei Li*) implied the absence of a tightly unified party organization at birth.

Furthermore, Chen Duxiu and Li Dazhao also had considerable differences of opinion on the revolutionary role of the workers and peasants. Chen Duxiu held that peasants were backward and their forces were scattered. Therefore, according to him, it was difficult for peasants to participate in the revolutionary movement, whereas the progressive urban elements should spearhead the movement. On the contrary, Li Dazhao stressed the importance of the peasantry who constituted more than 80 percent of the population. He believed that peasants were important because agriculture was still the basis of the national economy. He urged young intellectuals to go to the villages to liberate the peasants and stimulate their revolutionary energies. The newborn party supported Chen Duxiu's position. Years later, it initiated several urban uprisings, but all failed. After Li Dazhao was executed in 1927 by Zhang Zuolin, a warlord in North China, Mao Zedong was inspired by his mentor's ideas, and thus carried on the peasant struggle and put this idea into practice. This proved to be an effective way for the CCP to gain military and political power during the following 20 years.

Temple of Heaven, Beijing

CHAPTER 10

THE NATIONALIST-COMMUNIST COLLABORATION

10.1 DR. SUN YATSEN AND THE CHINESE NATIONALIST PARTY

In the wake of the May Fourth Movement, Chinese intellectuals saw the hope of Chinese revolution in the Bolshevik victory in Russia. While leftist intellectuals such as Chen Duxiu and Li Dazhao initiated the first Chinese Communist movement, Dr. Sun Yatsen, father of the Chinese Revolution, was, to a great extent inspired by Leninism and the successful example of the Russian Revolution. Disappointed by the lack of unity and discipline within his party, Sun decided to reorganize the party for the third time, after the Soviet model, despite the previous two unsuccessful attempts — from the Chinese United League to the Chinese Revolutionary Party (*Zhongguo gemingdang*) in 1914, and to the Chinese Nationalist Party (*Zhongguo guomindang*) (GMD) in 1919. Neither of them had fulfilled Dr. Sun's purpose of promoting discipline and cooperation among his party members. The Nationalist Party had never been a tightly integrated structure, and obstructions such as Chen Jiongming's mutiny in 1922 and the southwestern military governors' disavowal of allegiance still occurred frequently.

The second reason for Dr. Sun's third party reform is that he saw the imperialist nature of the Western powers, and therefore turned to seek Soviet aid instead for the National Revolution. Dr. Sun's Nationalist Party had long been disfavored by the foreign powers seeking their interests in China. As early as 1913, they had patronized Yuan Shikai with a loan of £25 million to crush the Second Revolution. In addition, the British minister supplied Yuan with munitions and barred Dr. Sun and Huang Xing, another major revolutionary leader, from landing in Hong Kong. After Yuan's death, they continued to support various warlords, and actually became the hands behind the curtain fomenting civil strife. At the Paris Peace Conference, the Western powers unilaterally decided to transfer Shandong to Japan, while ignoring China's rightful desire for the return of sovereignty. This further disillusioned the Chinese revolutionaries.

The success of the Bolshevik Revolution, the Soviet offer of friendship, and abolition of the unequal treaties gave new hope to Dr. Sun. Blaming himself for lacking organization and inadequate indoctrination within the party, he was eager to learn from the Soviet experience. However, the Leninst government did not consider Dr. Sun and the GMD as the first choice for cooperation. It was not until the Soviet delegation's failure in 1920 to negotiate treaties, first with the legal government in Beijing and then with the powerful warlord Wu Peifu, that Dr. Sun was "rediscovered" by the Soviets.

In the spring of 1921, Dr. Sun first met in Guangxi with the Comintern's Dutch agent, H. Maring, who was most impressed with Sun's nationalist spirit and ideas on revolution. Dr. Sun was also gratified to hear about the Soviet's new economic policy. This meeting set the stage for the first Nationalist-Communist collaboration that followed.

10.2 THE NATIONALIST-COMMUNIST UNITED FRONT (1923-1927)

The first Nationalist-Communist United Front, or more accurately, the Soviet-GMD-CCP cooperation, was formally launched in 1922. It was marked by the arrival of Adolf Joffe in China, who was sent by the Comintern to negotiate the details of collaboration with Dr. Sun. After lengthy talks with Joffe, Dr. Sun decided on the policy of "alliance with the Soviets; admission of the Communists" (*Lian-E rong-Gong*), which was approved at a Nationalist Conference in Shanghai later on, and then became the cardinal principle in the reorganization of the GMD. Also at that conference, Chen Duxiu was included in a nine-man committee in charge of the reorganization, and a manifesto drafted by Hu Hanmin was announced on January 1, 1923. In addition, on January 12 under the instruction of the Comintern, the Chinese Communists entered the GMD as individuals rather than as a bloc, and they agreed to acknowledge the GMD as the leading and central force of the National Revolution.

The results of the Sun-Joffe negotiations led to a four-point joint manifesto on January 26, 1923, signifying the final establishment of the collaboration:

(1) It was not possible to carry out Communism or the Soviet system in China at present;

(2) The Soviet government reaffirmed its earlier announcement of September 27, 1920, which proclaimed its renunciation of special rights and privileges in China;

(3) A mutual understanding was reached with regard to the future administration and reorganization of the Chinese Eastern Railway;

(4) The Soviets disavowed any imperialist intentions or policies in Outer Mongolia.

As promised, the Soviets sent Mikhail Borodin and some 40 advisers to help Sun reorganize the GMD. Dr. Sun also dispatched his entrusted young general Chiang Kaishek to study military arts in the Soviet Union. Upon Chiang's return, he was immediately commissioned to found the Whampoa Military Academy outside Guangzhou, which was the starting point for the GMD to have its own standing force.

Each of the three parties involved had different analyses and expectations:

(1) *From Dr. Sun's Point of View* — There were three things that he considered: (i) He had noticed the founding of the CCP and the fervent nationalism among the younger generation after the May Fourth Movement, and in circumstances so favorable towards Marxism, he decided to use these new elements in his aged revolutionary alliance for the best interests of his party; (ii) Obviously, Soviet support was a major goal, yet he showed enough practical statesmanship to refuse the substitution of Communism for his Three People's Principles, and the power of leadership was tightly held in the hands of the GMD; and (iii) He proceeded with an intention to utilize the CCP's ties with the workers, peasants, and the masses in order to ensure the communists a role within his organization. He also understood very well that any rapid, independent growth of the CCP under Soviet aegis, with its commitment to class

struggle, would ultimately undermine his own course of National Revolution if he did not absorb this growth into the GMD and assimilate it in time. Lastly, Dr. Sun was also concerned about possible Soviet aid to warlords who were opposed to him.

(2) *From the Soviets' Point of View* — The real intention of Moscow was to graft the young CCP onto the established body of the GMD so that it could subvert it from within, assert proletarian hegemony, and squeeze out the rightists like "lemons."

(3) *From the CCP's Point of View* — At first the CCP leaders, especially Chen Duxiu, were reluctant to let the Communists enter the GMD. But soon, under Soviet coaching, they perceived the utility of this course very well, and prepared to use the GMD as a base to expand their influence. In order to pacify some conservative GMD members averse to the merger with the CCP, Li Dazhao tactfully declared on January 28, 1924, during the first National Congress of the GMD, that CCP members had entered the GMD to devote themselves to the revolution, not for advancing the Communist cause. However, the fact that they gave the party's interests priority and formed "a bloc within the GMD" at last became the basis for a GMD-CCP split.

In one sense, the Nationalist-Communist collaboration was a marriage of convenience, each party needing but distrusting the other. Dr. Sun might have had some misgivings about this, but miscalculation of the difficulties involved made him assume that the CCP could be dissolved within his party.

10.3 DEATH OF DR. SUN YATSEN AND THE POLITICS OF SUCCESSION

Upon the completion of party reorganization, Dr. Sun could not wait any longer to launch the Northern Expedition, an undertaking that would be dedicated to wiping out the warlords and frustrating their foreign patrons. However, by March 12, 1925, this ambition was left to Dr. Sun's successors because of his untimely death due to illness. For a long time, Sun's stature and prestige had been the crucial element connecting the GMD and CCP. Now the soul of this collaboration was gone, and the long-covered tensions between these two groups came to the surface.

Since no one within the GMD had enough prestige to inherit Dr. Sun's political mantle alone, the leadership fell onto two people: Wang Jingwei and Hu Hanmin, the left- and right-wing leaders of the GMD, respectively. In the meantime, a third power was emerging with decisive military strength; its leader, Chiang Kaishek, was the superintendent of the Whampoa Military Academy, and was in charge of developing an officer corps to staff the new party army. Another important figure was Dr. Sun's confidant Liao Zhongkai, who served as the chief party representative in the Academy. All orders and regulations in the Academy and the party army had to be countersigned by the superintendent and Liao. However, after the assassination of Liao Zhongkkai in August 1925, there was no one left to constrain Chiang Kaishek's absolute rule of the military. Meanwhile, Communist influence was also developing. At that time, the young Zhou Enlai had already been made deputy head of the Political Education Department.

As the Whampoa cadets rapidly became a powerful military factor, the GMD's forces grew strong enough to secure Guangzhou from hostile powers. During this period, several local uprisings were successfully suppressed, and the rebel governor Chen Jiongming and various southwestern warlords were frustrated and driven out of power. On July 1, 1925, a Nationalist Government was established to challenge the Beijing warlord government, and Wang Jingwei was elected president. Nevertheless, the power struggle among different factions within the GMD had just begun, along with mounting antagonsim with the CCP. It was not until Chiang Kaishek established his own stature through the Northern Expedition that the divided party was reunited into one structure, and the first Nationalist-Communist Collaboration was formally aborted in 1927.

CHAPTER 11

THE RISE OF CHIANG KAISHEK

11.1 CHIANG KAISHEK AND THE NORTHERN EXPEDITION

As a young general, Chiang Kaishek gained the confidence of revolutionary leader Dr. Sun Yatsen by saving his life on one occasion. Chiang soon became Sun's trusted military leader, and in August of 1923 he was sent to the Soviet Union for three months to study the Soviet military system, the political indoctrination of the Red Army, and the methods of discipline in the Bolshevik Party. Upon his return, Chiang was commissioned to set up a military academy at Whampoa, right outside Guangzhou. From 1924 onwards, Chiang Kaishek was the highest commander in charge of the Nationalist Party military. Chiang's experience in the Soviet Union not only taught him military strategies, but also made him believe that communism was not suitable for China, and that something was terribly wrong about the first united front between the Chinese Nationalist Party and the Chinese Communist Party.

After the reorganization of the party and the united front between the GMD and CCP, Sun Yatsen was eager to resume his plan of a Northern Expedition to wipe out the warlords and factionalism that plagued China. Unfortunately, Sun died before this could be achieved. The united front's weaknesses emerged and a political struggle ensued between Wang Jingwei, a Nationalist with sympathies to the Communists, and Hu Hanmin, a die-hard Nationalist. All military power still rested with Chiang, who was in charge of developing an officer corps to staff the new party army. All orders and regulations in the academy and the party army had to be countersigned by a party representative in order for the superintendent to validate and enforce the order. Sure enough, the cadets under Chiang's control soon became extremely powerful, and in October 1924 they suppressed the Hong Kong-Guangzhou Merchants' Volunteers Uprising, as well as several southwestern warlords.

On July 1, 1925, the Nationalist government was officially established at Guangzhou, with Wang Jingwei as acting president. One year later, Chiang Kaishek was appointed commander-in-chief of the National Revolutionary Army. With this powerful position, and 6,000 Whampoa cadets and 85,000 troops under his command, Chiang was convinced that the GMD was ready to embark on the Northern Expedition to wipe out the warlords. Thus, on July 27 they set out on their quest to rid China of warlords and factionalism, with the help of Soviet supplies and CCP advance agents who mobilized peasant and worker organizations. The Northern Expeditionary forces plowed their way from Guangzhou to Central China, winning control of Wuhan in September of 1926. Wang's GMD government moved to Wuhan, and the expeditionary forces moved onto Nanchang in November, Fuzhou in December, and finally Shanghai and Nanjing in March of 1927. In nine months, the southern half of China had been conquered, but the GMD-CCP split threatened to dissolve the party and interrupt the process of national unification.

11.2 THE PURGE OF COMMUNISTS BY CHIANG

Chiang's first break with the Communists came on March 20, 1926, with the "Warship *Zhongshan* Incident." The captain of the *Zhongshan*, a warship under Communist control, attempted to kidnap Chiang but failed. Chiang responded by dismissing the captain, all Soviet advisors, and party representatives in the First Army and its affiliated military establishments. Chiang's early suspicions of the Russians had been confirmed. Further open denunciation of the Communists came on May 15, 1926, when the GMD Central Executive Committee passed nine resolutions intended to completely limit Communist participation and leadership in the GMD. It was on these pretenses that Chiang had set out on the Northern Expedition with his forces in 1927. The easy defeat of the Shanghai-Nanjing financial circles gave him more determination to persecute the Communists.

When the GMD government moved from Guangzhou to Wuhan in January 1927, the CCP received an order from Stalin, actually dated November 30, 1926, instructing the Communists to intensify their political work in the revolutionary army, and improve their military knowledge. This was specifically called to strengthen CCP members in preparation for taking important positions within the united front and the military. The Wuhan government was primarily dominated by the GMD left wing, but Stalin wanted to make sure that the Communists' power grew within the organization. Organizations of workers and farmers were placed under the charge of the Communists, and they actively followed Stalin's orders. These groups tried to mobilize the masses in order to embarrass and attack the GMD rightists. At this point, Chiang had already set out on the expedition and was rapidly building a power base in Eastern and Southeastern China, but the evident threat of the Communists was becoming more and more apparent to him.

On April 10, 1927, a "purge committee" was organized to rid the Communists, and Chiang ordered the dissolution of the political department of the National Revolutionary Army. Only two days later, the persecution of the Communists began, first in Shanghai, then in Nanjing, Hangzhou, Fuzhou, Guangzhou, as well as in many other cities. Nationalist troops, police, and secret agents raided the underground Communist community and killed anyone whom they even slightly suspected of being a Communist. Because the Communists were caught off guard by Chiang's change in strategy, the bloodshed was tremendous, and thousands lost their lives. Most of the Communists' arms were confiscated and those that remained (specifically those that belonged to the underground Communists) were buried following Moscow's command to demonstrate cooperation with Chiang. Ironically, during this time Chiang continued to profess friendship with Moscow on the basis that his quarrels were only with the local Communists. Immense pressure from the Communists led the GMD Wuhan government under the direction of Wang to dismiss Chiang Kaishek from his post as commander-in-chief of the National Revolutionary Army.

11.3   CHIANG AND THE RE-UNIFICATION OF CHINA

Chiang was not bothered by his dismissal from the Wuhan government, for he knew that he had the power to continue the Northern Expedition without its support. On April 18, 1927, Chiang organized his own Nationalist government at Nanjing, with the help of Hu Hanmin, the die-hard Nationalist leader who had fought to be Sun's successor. Chiang successfully continued the Northern Expedition along the

Tianjin-Pukou Railway on June 2. The Wuhan government tried to counter Chiang's control by an expedition effort of its own; however, its mission failed because of warlords who refused to cooperate. With Chiang's increasing success, the Soviet leaders Trotsky and Stalin began to argue between themselves — Trotsky accused Stalin of flawed leadership in China. Trotsky also felt that Stalin's plan for China violated a cardinal principle of Leninism — specifically, the temporary agreement or alliance with bourgeois elements was permissible only if Communists retained their organizational independence and freedom of action. Trotsky felt that the GMD-CCP collaboration did not allow Communists freedom of action.

In the midst of the Trotsky-Stalin power struggle in Russia, Stalin, in dire need of a victory, sent a telegram on June 1, 1927, to the CCP. This telegram asked the CCP to, in effect, raise a separate army, transform Wuhan into a Communist regime, and select current GMD president Wang Jingwei to be in charge. Once Wang learned of the telegram (leaked to him by a Comintern agent by the name of M.N. Roy), he realized Stalin's true intentions: to destroy the GMD by inserting communism within the organization. Wang's Communist sympathies caused him to not retaliate immediately, but he began to break away from the Communists. Instead of instant retaliation, Wang took a practical approach and continued with Chiang's early attempts at limiting the CCP's membership and leadership within the GMD. This plan of a slow crackdown on the Communists was immediately aborted after the following incident.

On August 1, 1927, the Nanchang Uprising took place in which Communists rebelled in the name of the Nationalist Left Wing. This prompted Wang to order a complete liquidation of the Communists, and a re-structuring of the front organizations including the General Labor Union, Farmers'

Association, Women's Association, and the Merchants' Association. This mutual goal of eliminating Communist control reconciled the Nanjing and Wuhan governments. A special Central Committee was established at Nanjing to exercise the power of the party headquarters. Remarkably, on December 10, all differences between the Wuhan and Nanjing governments were reconciled. Chiang Kaishek was soon officially re-appointed to his position as commander-in-chief of the National Revolutionary Army. Wang went into exile in Japan.

The Wuhan government was officially dissolved in February 1928. Chiang immediately resumed the Northern Expedition, with the goal of capturing Beijing. At that time, Beijing was occupied by the Fengtian warlord, Zhang Zuolin. With Chiang Kaishek's arrival, Zhang immediately fled to Manchuria, thereby giving Chiang an easy opportunity to conquer the capital. Once in Manchuria, Zhang Zuolin was killed by the Japanese, who wanted to eliminate Chinese influence there. In a twist of irony, Zhang's son, Young Marshal Zhang Xueliang, pledged allegiance to the Nationalist government in July, and in December he renounced his regional control of Manchuria. With this action, he also accepted the Three People's Principles and the Nationalist government's flag.

Thus, early in 1929, the greater part of China was unified by Chiang Kaishek, after thirteen years of civil anarchy. Nanjing became the city for the new seat of government, and the old capital at Beijing was renamed Beiping, meaning "Northern Peace." The new government was dedicated to the fulfillment of Dr. Sun's legacy, which entailed the Three People's Principles, the Five-Power Constitution, the Fundamental Principles of National Reconstruction, and his deathbed admonition, "The revolution is not yet completed; comrades must strive on!" Internally, the new government promised democratic reconstruction and social reforms, while externally it promised to fight for the complete abolition of the unequal treaties and win China a position of equality with the world powers. However, the new government was not aware that its fight with the Communists was not over.

CHAPTER 12

THE CHINESE COMMUNIST REVOLUTION UNDER ATTACK

12.1 MAO ZEDONG IN OPPOSITION

After the split with the GMD in 1927, the Communists were divided into two separate groups. One was the party's Central Politburo, which fell under the leadership of Moscow-trained Chinese Communists working underground in Shanghai. The other half advocated an independent course led by Mao Zedong in the countryside of Hunan and Jiangxi. While the Politburo was using the Comintern tactics of strikes, sabotage, and uprisings in the cities, Mao organized peasant support and expanded CCP-controlled areas away from GMD control.

Believing that the Chinese revolution was at high tide, Stalin pushed the strategies of armed uprisings, seizure of power, and the establishment of local Soviet-style regimes. After Stalin defeated Trotsky, who advocated a conciliatory line in dealing with Chiang Kaishek, he ordered the CCP to carry out armed insurrections. However, the Nanchang Uprising on August 1, 1927, was a failure for Stalin's strategy. On August 7, a radical leadership reform took place, resulting in the dismissal of Chen Duxiu; his position was filled by Qu Qiubai, who became secretary-general of the Central Politburo. Li Lisan was placed in charge of propaganda. Under the advice of B. Lominadze, the new Comintern representative, these leaders accepted Moscow's advocacy for armed insurrections and the creation of Soviets in China.

Meanwhile, Mao entered Hunan and instigated the Autumn Harvest Uprising of September 7, 1927. Rebellious peasants destroyed sections of the Guangzhou-Hankou Railway, seized control of a number of places, assassinated landlords, and carried out abortive land reforms. However, Mao's first uprising was a failure, since it came under attack by government troops; this event forced him to flee to Jinggangshan to regroup his forces, and cost him the Politburo membership.

While Moscow's attempts to intensify the urban uprising failed one after another, Mao's activity at Jinggangshan assumed more importance in the countryside. Joined by Zhu De, Chen Yi, the three combined forces on January 23, 1928, the Fourth Red army was formed, with Zhu as commander and Mao as party representative, thus marking the birth of Zhu-Mao leadership. In July, they moved their headquarters to Ruijin, Jiangxi and established a Soviet regime. The Jiangxi base became the second Communist center besides a base in Shaanxi, which was created by Liu Zhidan and Gao Gang. It operated in the border area, outside the jurisdiction of the CCP Central Politburo.

In July 1928, the CCP Sixth Party Congress, which was held in Moscow, coincided with the Comintern's International

Congress to eliminate Trotskyite influences. Chen Duxiu was condemned for his "rightist opportunism," and Qu Qiubai for his "leftist deviance." The Congress called for (1) the overthrow of the Nationalist government and its military power; (2) the establishment of Soviets in China; (3) land revolution and confiscation of landlords' holdings; and (4) the unification of China through the imperialists' expulsion. Xiang Zhongfa and Li Lisan were elected as secretary-general and director of propaganda, respectively. However, after the failure to seize Changsha, Pavel Mif, the Comintern representative who resented Li's iron control of the party, asked Moscow to dismiss him. The Comintern and the Russian-returned Student Clique launched a campaign against Li as well. Thus, Li was sent to Moscow for criticism as a result of Stalin's failure. The party leadership fell to Wang Ming and Bo Gu, the heads of the CCP international wing consisting of 28 returned students from the Sun Yat-sen University in Moscow. With Mif's support, this "Twenty-eight Bolsheviks" or "China's Stalin Section" took over the Politburo in January 1931.

12.2 THE CHINESE SOVIET REPUBLIC (1931-1934)

Mao and Zhu developed their independent activity by organizing the peasants and establishing Soviet areas in Jiangxi and Hunan. They practiced guerrilla warfare and initiated an egalitarian land revolution by distributing land to the rich and poor peasants equally. They developed a self-sufficient territorial base relying neither on the help and guidance of the Comintern, nor the party leaders at Shanghai. The CCP Central Politburo never approved of Mao's activity, but Moscow simply tolerated it due to the failure of the other CCP uprisings. While Mao's power and independence were growing, the state of the party central organization was contrastingly plagued by unstable leadership, lack of financial support from the Soviet Union, and Nationalist persecution. The GMD arrested the

Communist secret service chief in Hankou, which led to the capture and execution of Xiang Zhongfa on June 24, 1931, and put party fortunes at a low ebb.

Accordingly, Mao invited members of the Politburo to attend the First All-China Congress of Soviets held in Ruijin on November 7, 1931. The 28 Bolsheviks arrived in Mao's capital with the intent to repudiate his conduct by condemning his failure to adopt a strong class and mass line, his guerrilla tactics, and attitude towards the land revolution. However, the Maoists completely dominated the Congress. Thus, Mao was elected chairman of the Central Executive Committee of the All-China Soviet Government, and held on to his position as Chief Political Commissar of the First Front Red Army. Mao's government absorbed a number of former party members and left out so-called Bolsheviks during the distribution of offices. Mao increasingly won recognition for his activity through his realistic strategies: (1) peasant mass support; (2) his party and government apparatus; (3) an independent military force; (4) a secure territorial base far away from the GMD control; and (5) self-sufficiency. The Bolsheviks retained control of the Politburo, continuing to obstruct Mao and put him in opposition to the CCP central organization.

The Bolsheviks and the Maoists differed on a number of issues. On the issue of land reform, Mao favored the equal distribution of all grades of lands to both poor and rich peasants, but the Politburo members insisted on complete deprivation of the landlords and relocation of land to favor the poor at the expense of the rich. On military strategy, Mao chose mobile guerrilla tactics, while the Politburo preferred positional warfare. On the issue of Japanese aggression, Mao was ready to form a United Front and a coalition army of all military forces, but the Politburo refused to collaborate with reformist groups and argued for the rapid expansion of the Red army.

After the dismissal of Soviet military advisors in 1927, the GMD under Chiang's guidance obtained German aid and developed a German-style Central army. From 1930 to 1934, Chiang launched five Campaigns of Encirclement and Suppression against the Communists. Although the first four campaigns from December 19, 1930, to April 29, 1933, ended in failure, they stirred a critical power struggle among the Communists. In late 1932 or early 1933, Bo Gu and other CCP Politburo members arrived in Ruijin with Li De (Otto Braun), a Comintern military advisor, to discredit Mao and replace his men in the army and the party. To criticize Mao's egalitarian approach, they eliminated the landlords, attacked rich peasants, neutralized middle peasants, and allied poor peasants and landless laborers with the party. Funds from the campaign were used for the Red Army's expansion. Finally, Mao reluctantly accepted the fact that he could not dispute the need for funds to support and expand the army. In the meantime, the Nationalists were organizing the fifth encirclement campaign starting with 700,000 men, and slowly but steadily they adopted a "strategically offensive but tactically defensive" posture that constructed fortresses and cut off outside supplies to the Communist areas.

At this time, Mao faced an extremely critical situation both from Nationalist attacks and from attempts by Politburo members to destroy him. He almost lost his control over the Chinese Communist movement at the Second All-China Soviet Congress. Although he was re-elected chairman of the Soviet government in January 1934, he lost his power in the Central Executive Committee to the Bolsheviks and his chairmanship was reduced to only an honorary title. Zhang Wentian of the Bolsheviks took over Mao's chairmanship of the Council of People's Commissars. The coup de grace came in July 1934, when Bo Gu at Ruijin and Wang Ming in Moscow, put Mao on probation and barred him from party meetings. He was placed under house arrest at Yudu for three months and was only released in October when the Long March began.

12.3   THE LONG MARCH TO POWER

The Communist defeat by the GMD Fifth Encirclement Campaign was the result of Li De's choice of positional warfare over Mao's guerrilla combat. The Red Army suffered losses throughout the first half of 1934. On October 15, the Long March officially began with 85,000 soldiers, 15,000 government and party officials, and 35 women or wives of high-ranking leaders. The Bolsheviks left behind a number of Maoists and the ex-party leaders to defend the base. On November 10, Ruijin fell to the Nationalists.

In the beginning, a three-man Military Group composed of Li De, Bo Gu, and Zhou Enlai directed the Long March. However, troop confidence was very low due to frustration with Li and Bo's leadership and the heavy losses of the Communists in the GMD fifth campaign. Resentment at Li's arrogance and high-handed manner of operation coupled with Bo's conspiratorial tendencies, aroused the need to remove them from power. Wang Jiaxiang, a key member of the Politburo and director of the Political Department of the Red Army, expressed this feeling and discussed his concerns with Mao, who agreed but urged caution and careful preparation for a confrontation. Wang was able to lobby and win the support of several key officials, including Zhang Wentian, Zhu De, and Zhou Enlai, vice-chairman of the Central Revolutionary Military Council. Two trends became apparent at a Politburo Conference in Liping on December 18, 1934, and as a result, the majority of the Politburo desired a change in leadership and Mao's star was rising as a symbol of the correct line in opposition to Li and Bo.

On January 15-18, 1935, after the Red Army reached Zunyi in Guizhou province on January 7, the so-called Zunyi Conference was organized with the participants of all powerful leaders in the Party and the Red Army. Mao delivered a blistering attack on Li and Bo's mistaken leadership of leftist adventurism, which was held responsible for the CCP's defeat in the Fifth Campaign, the loss of the base area, and the near destruction of the Red Army. Wang, Zhang, Zhou, and Zhu spoke out in support of Mao. Li and Bo had to resign. Mao became a member of the Politburo Standing Committee and an assistant to Zhou Enlai in military affairs. On February 5, Zhang Wentian replaced Bo Gu as the person with overall responsibility. In March, a new three-man Military Group was formed with Mao, Zhou, and Wang as members. Among the three, Mao was the real power. Shortly thereafter, with Zhang's help, Mao won absolute control of the military, which became his power base.

The Zunyi Conference was a giant step in Mao's quest for supreme power. However, the party elder Zhang Guotao refused to accept its results; he questioned the choice of northern Shaanxi as the last stop for the Long March and argued moving south or west in the direction of Xikang or Tibet. A split occurred, and Zhang and his troops left Mao's group. In October 1935, Mao's group reached Wuqizhen in Baoan County. At the end of this 25,000 *li* (about 6,000 miles) Long March, only 8,000 of Mao's forces remained. In December 1936, CCP headquarters was moved to Yan'an where Mao was the de facto leader of the Chinese Communist movement. He rebuilt the party and the army around himself, and began to undertake the task of theoretical writing. In 1938, a Soviet encyclopedia recognized him as the leader of the CCP. He was selected chairman of the preparatory committee for the convocation of the Seventh Party Congress in 1945. Mao's victory was complete. He became chairman of the CCP Central Committee, the Politburo, the Secretariat, and the Military Commission. His thought was accepted as the guiding principle of the party.

CHAPTER 13

JAPAN'S ATTACK ON CHINA

13.1   THE INVASION OF MANCHURIA (1931)

Manchuria, located in Northeast China, is known for its abundant agricultural products and mineral resources. Japan coveted Manchuria ever since its defeat of China in 1895. Its victory in the Russo-Japanese war (1904-1905) won Japan the former concessions of Russia in Manchuria. Japan's annexation of Korea in 1910 opened the door for a Japanese conquest of Manchuria. In the years 1912, 1916, and 1928 the Japanese schemed to foment a "Manchuria-Mongolia Autonomous Movement," but only met with failure. The Japanese Kwantung army, located in southern Manchuria and virtually free from homeland control, supported the idea of further military action in Manchuria. The army then took upon itself the task of wresting Manchuria from China. In 1928, two key strategists in the Kwantung army, Lt. Colonel Ishiwara Kanji and Colonel Itagaki Seishiro, became the ideological and political mentors of the army and openly advocated the occupation of Manchuria. To justify this occupation, they argued that 30 million people in Manchuria were eagerly awaiting Japanese liberation from the misrule of warlords and greedy bureaucrats.

At the beginning of the 1930s, with a civil war brewing in China, and the international powers preoccupied with the Depression and economic hardships of their own, the Japanese felt the time was ripe for their conquest of Manchuria. Japanese military leaders began to emerge as powerful forces in the national government. Although Tokyo's government set a target year of 1932 for the occupation of Manchuria, the Kwantung army did not wish to wait any longer. On September 18, 1931, a bomb exploded on the Southern Manchurian railway track outside of Mukden (Shenyang). In the meantime, a messenger from Tokyo had been dispatched to Manchuria to inform and warn the army of its need to wait until the time was right. However, Kwantung soldiers claimed that the Chinese had set off the bomb, and that when they attempted to investigate the incident they were fired upon. The following morning, the city of Mukden was attacked by the Japanese Kwantung army.

Both the Tokyo headquarters and Commander Honjo Shigeru knew of the contrived invasion plot, but took no action to stop it. Subsequently, they allowed field grade officers of the Kwantung army to take the fate of Japan into their own hands and lead her down the road of militarism, conquest, and ultimately destruction. The Kwantung army continued to advance on its own with complete disregard of any orders from Tokyo. On December 10, 1931, the League of Nations decided to investigate the situation in Manchuria. When the League criticized Japan for Manchuria's degenerate state, it withdrew from the organization. Without support from the U.S., the League of Nations was virtually powerless. Within five months time, the Japanese army completely overran Manchuria and created a puppet state known as Manchukuo on March 9,

1932. The last Qing emperor Puyi was placed on the throne on March 1, 1934. Although the Japanese had completed their goal of conquering Manchuria, they soon began to visualize conquering the whole of China Proper.

13.2   THE INVASION OF CHINA PROPER (1937)

Young officers of the Kwantung army were eager to strike before China became too strong, and were encouraged by the easy conquest of Manchuria, the lack of international sanctions, and the rise of Nazism and Facism. However, what the Japanese intended to be a short war to conquer northern China turned out to be a long war of attrition, which lasted until 1945. The young officers were the self-appointed saviors of the country, and vowed to effect a "Showa Restoration." This restoration would re-establish a direct relationship between Showa the emperor, Hirohito, and the people at large through the military. Nothing was allowed to undermine the prestige and position of the army.

Throughout the years 1932-36, the militarists rose steadily in national politics until they totally eclipsed civilian government through coups and assassinations. On May 15, 1932, the militarists attempted a coup and assassinated the finance minister, governor of the Bank of Japan, and the Premier, Inukai Tsuyoshi. The next few years were filled with conflicts within the army, which generated instability and turmoil. Furthermore, in January 1936, the minister of finance slashed the army budget, inspiring outrage in the army. On February 26, a group of young officers and 1,400 soldiers seized control of central Tokyo. The coup was suppressed, but Admiral Okada Keisuke resigned, and Hirota Koki took over the realm of government. Hirota was well known for his extremist connections and aggressive policy for China. Preceding Hirota's succession into the government, the Japanese in north China sponsored an autonomous movement of the five provinces of Hebei, Chahaer, Suiyuan, Shanxi, and Shandong. It was not long afterwards that they created an Eastern Hebei Autonomous Council, and the whole of north China began to look like a second Manchuria.

During the summer of 1936, Hirota opened up negotiations with China with five specific goals in mind: (1) end anti-Japanese activities in China; (2) have China recognize Japan's special position in the north; (3) facilitate Sino-Japanese collaboration against communism; (4) promote Sino-Japanese economic cooperation; and (5) place Japanese advisors in all branches of the Chinese government. Negotiations broke down in December 1936, and these were soon followed by the fall of Hirota's government. A general named Hayashi Senjuro took Hirota's position, and chose a rapprochement policy towards the war in China. However, his efforts to compromise ultimately failed and he was soon replaced by Prince Konoe Fumimaro. The administration under the prince was completely dominated by the military, the most notorious general of whom was Tojo Hideki. Tojo strongly advocated the application of force against China, and it was under his command that World War II officially began.

On July 7, 1937, during a field exercise outside of Beiping, Japanese soliders fabricated the Marco Polo Bridge Incident. Upon hearing a shot fired, Japanese soldiers demanded to enter the nearby city of Wanping under the pretext of searching for a missing soldier. The Chinese refused their entry, and soon the Japanese soldiers bombarded the city. The incident is marked as the official start of the war, since soon afterwards Japanese soldiers poured into northern China and wreaked havoc wherever they went. By late July, Beiping and Tianjin had been seized. A second front opened in Shanghai on August 13, where Chiang Kaishek's soldiers managed to stall the Japanese for three months. In reality, Japan had expected to seize north China within three months, but the brief and somewhat artificial United Front between the GMD and CCP helped to delay its conquest. The delay only served to infuriate the Japanese, thus precipitating the massacre that occurred in the next city of conquest, Nanjing.

Once Chiang Kaishek learned of the fall of Shanghai, he evacuated the city of Nanjing, and moved his headquarters up the Yangzi River to Chongqing. The incident at Nanjing, also known as the "Rape of Nanjing," left more than 100,000 civilians, including women and children, dead. The exact extent of the massacre is debated even today, as many argue that some 300,000 civilians may have actually been murdered. The rape and mutilation of Chinese women continues to haunt the Chinese today. After the massacre, the Japanese moved toward Xuzhou, an important communication junction. The conquest of this city led them to Wuhan in 1938, where it took over four and a half months to defeat the Chinese defenders. This marked the end of the first phase of war.

13.3 WARTIME CHINA

During the early years of the war, a number of important developments took place within the GMD and the government. In April of 1938, a convocation of the GMD Provisional National Congress took place in Wuhan, during which the congress adopted four major resolutions: (1) the creation of a new post of Director-General as the party leader; (2) the creation of a Three People's Principles Youth Corps to train young men as a basic force in the war; (3) the creation of a People's Political Council to replace the National Defense Advisory Council; and (4) the adoption of an "Outline of Resistance and Reconstruction." In Wuhan during the following July, an inaugural meeting between the CCP and GMD took place and the parties discussed the commitment to a national front. Subsequently, on September 22, 1937, a manifesto entitled, "Together We Confront the National Crisis," was issued by the CCP. Mao Zedong and other Communist leaders were elected to the People's Political Council in 1938 as a symbol of goodwill towards the GMD-CCP rapprochement. However, the alliance was ill fated.

Mao Zedong and the Communists mapped out a three-stage strategy to exploit the United Front to their full advantage. The United Front was seen as an organ through which the CCP could carry out the orders of the Comintern, be free from Nationalist persecution, and build up strength during the war with Japan. The growing tension between the two political parties was intensified by the rapidly shifting international alignments. On January 5, 1941, a major clash between the communist New Fourth army and the Nationalist 40th division all but destroyed the United Front. Throughout the remainder of the war, although the Chinese managed to stall the Japanese in a few areas, the communist problem was not resolved and civil war became almost immanent. Furthermore, the Yan'an period of wartime resistance (1937-1945) provided Mao and the CCP with much needed time to restructure the party and the army, organize the masses, and develop new social, political, and economic institutions. This period was of seminal importance to the development of Chinese communism.

From the outbreak of the war in July 1937, to the Japanese attack on Pearl Harbor in December 1941, China fought alone. The Soviet Union was the only country that offered China substantial material aid. The outbreak of the war in Europe in September 1939 completely altered the foreign aid picture. The Allied Powers established a China-Burma-India theater of war with Chiang Kaishek as supreme commander of the China theater. Tensions soon arose between the American military advisor Joseph Stillwell and Chiang. The quarrel strained relations between the two countries, as Stillwell pushed Chiang to take a more active stance towards fighting the Japanese. Furthermore, the Yalta conference of 1945 only increased the strain on a U.S.-China friendship. The Yalta conference brought together the big three powers to fix the terms of Soviet entry into the war. At the conference, Stalin agreed to enter the war within two or three months after Germany's defeat in exchange for the guarantees of its privileges in China and Manchuria, which had been taken by the Japanese at the start of the war. The U.S. agreed, but once the Chinese learned of its betrayal they were furious. The war was brought to a close a few months later when, in August of 1945, the United States dropped atomic bombs on Hiroshima and Nagasaki.

On August 14, 1945, the Japanese emperor issued an imperial rescript to end the war, and China emerged victorious. The Chinese were hopeful for a period of peace and reconstruction, since the war had left them with several consequences: (1) a new order in Asia with China replacing Japan as the leading power; (2) Nationalist exhaustion since the war had caused massive casualties and debt among the Nationalist government and its support; (3) economic distress was tremendous due to the chronic deficit spending and inflation during the war; and (4) psychological weariness overtook the Chinese people, who longed for peace and recuperation, and they subsequently blamed the government and party in power for the civil war that was to ensue. The war with Japan had left China exhausted and weak.

CHAPTER 14

CIVIL WAR AND THE COMMUNIST VICTORY

14.1 THE CIVIL WAR BETWEEN THE NATIONALISTS AND COMMUNISTS

The civil war between the Chinese Nationalists and Communists started with expanding their militia and power bases right after the end of World War II. Following the Japanese surrender, both the GMD and CCP forces strived to be the first to move into former Japanese occupied territories to accept enemy arms and supplies. At that moment, the Communists seemed to enjoy a geographical advantage, with one million regular troops and two million militiamen situated in North, South, and Central China, while the Nationalist forces were scattered along the frontier battlefield and throughout Western China.

To protect the fruits of victory from falling into Communist hands, Chiang Kaishek asked the Japanese to hold out against non-Nationalist troops. Denouncing Chiang's action as "beneficial to Japanese invaders and traitors," Zhu De, commander-in-chief of the People's Liberation Army (PLA), directly asked the Japanese to surrender to the Communists. However, the United States was undoubtedly on the GMD's side. Upon Chiang's request, it helped to airlift and sealift half a million Nationalist troops to the various occupied areas. In addition, Washington's General Order No. 1 to Tokyo explicitly required that the surrender be made to Chiang Kaishek and his representatives. With American assistance and Japanese cooperation, the GMD government seized nearly all the important cities, while the CCP temporarily retreated to the countryside. The Communists gained control of the vast areas of rural North China, and Soviet aid was hoped for soon.

Soviet forces had swept into Manchuria by August 8, 1945. With amazing speed, they kept moving south even after the Japanese surrender on August 14. Soviet troops penetrated deep into Rehe and Chahaer, facilitating the entry of the CCP forces into Manchuria. Although the Soviets turned over to the Chinese Communists considerable quantities of Japanese arms, they did not let them take over Manchuria.

In order to resolve these knotty problems, Mao Zedong flew to Chongqing on August 28, 1945, at Chiang's invitation to negotiate. The little progress achieved during the meeting was partly due to the passive role American envoy General Patrick Hurley played, but for the most part it was because both parties refused to compromise on important issues. Both Chiang and Mao still had a lack of trust in each other and were afraid of being duped if they agreed to a truce. On October 10, there was a final communiqué issued by Chiang and Mao, agreeing on no more than the convocation of a Political Consultative Conference. Upon Mao's return, he called upon his followers to mobilize the masses and expand the PLA in order to make "peace" and build a new China.

With the adoption of a new China policy — namely to assist the Nationalist government without an American military involvement — Washington appointed General George C. Marshall as the new ambassador to China. Arriving in China in mid-December 1945, Marshall won cooperation from both sides at first. Because of his mediation, two impressive results were achieved: (1) A Political Consultative Conference took place between January 10 and 31, with representatives from the GMD, CCP, Democratic League, and other independent parties; (2) An agreement regarding the relative strength of the GMD and the CCP forces, and integration of them into a national army was approached on February 25, 1946. It seemed that these achievements were politically beneficial to the CCP, but militarily favorable to the GMD. However, during Marshall's short leave of absence in the U.S., the extremists in the two parties quickly stirred up local military clashes, which soon grew into large-scale fighting in April 1946. On July 4, the Nationalist government unilaterally announced that it would convoke the National Assembly in November, which violated the PCC resolution and was boycotted by the CCP and the Democratic League because it was seen as "illegal." Then Mao formally called for a war of self-defense.

14.2   THE NATIONALIST RETREAT TO TAIWAN

In the early phase of the civil war, GMD forces encountered a chain of victories. At the end of the first year, the Communist "liberated areas" had shrunk on a large scale. Mao and the CCP leaders evacuated Yan'an and fled into hiding. A National Assembly was convened by the Nationalists on November 15, 1946, and adopted a new constitution. Chiang Kaishek was elected president of the Republic on April 19,

1948. However, Chiang did not come to his peak of power until a critical stage in the fighting.

As the reconquered areas increased, more soldiers were assigned to garrison duties, and the actual fighting force reduced correspondingly. In contrast, with a steadily growing quantity of manpower, the Communists went on a general counteroffensive in the second half of 1947. The severest crack came when Chiang's 470,000 best troops were destroyed in Manchuria, nearly striking a mortal blow to the morale of the entire GMD army. Almost simultaneously, the Communists won on the Jinan, Tianjin, and Xuzhou battlefields. By the time the Battle of Huai-Hai — a major campaign in the Civil War — was over in January 1949, the main military force of the GMD had perished.

If it were not for the eight-year China War, which completely exhausted the Nationalists militarily, financially, and spiritually, China might be different today. Yet, the poor military strategies and economic administration of the GMD had a large impact on its downfall. Chiang's stubborn decision to send his main forces to Manchurian cities and the isolated islands besieged by the sea of countryside dominated by the CCP, as well as his ill-fated order to take Yan'an and pursue the fleeing Communist leaders to the strategically unimportant mountainous Northwest, gradually had the GMD forces drained of strength. Much worse, financial mismanagement led to galloping inflation, which destroyed the livelihood of hundreds of millions of Chinese and totally discredited the government. During the brief span from August 1948 to April 1949, note issues increased by 4,524 times, and the Shanghai price index rose an astronomical 135,742 times. Moreover, Nationalist officials returning to the Japanese-occupied areas treated the inhabitants contemptuously, as if they were conquerors and the people were disloyal citizens and traitors. It is no wonder that the majority was not averse to, and even looked forward to, a change in administration.

In the Beiping-Tianjin battle in December 1948, General Fu Zuoyi, the famous Nationalist defender who had earlier defeated Communist forces in Suiyuan, gave up all resistance when his defense plans were stolen by a Communist agent operating in his headquarters. With 200,000 troops, he surrendered to the CCP; thus the old capital, Beiping, the occupation of which had long been the symbol of legitimate administration, fell into the hands of the Communists. Trying to initiate negotiations with the CCP, the Nationalist government forced Chiang Kaishek to resign in January 1949, and Vice-President Li Zongren took over. But it was too late either to compromise or to pursue any kind of reform. In December 1949, two months after the foundation of the People's Republic of China, the Nationalist government had to flee from Chongqing to Taiwan. Chiang soon returned to the presidency, and set up a regime in exile on December 8, which eventually included some two million soldiers and GMD members who had escaped the Communist regime on the mainland.

Chiang's defeat by the Communists could not be separated from the passive U.S.-China policy. Instead of picking mainland China, Washington chose Japan after World War II as its base in Asia to influence the Pacific area. Thus, the Nationalist government was put into a less strategically important position, and was to some extent "abandoned" by America.

14.3 FOUNDING OF THE PEOPLE'S REPUBLIC OF CHINA (1949)

On October 1, 1949, Mao Zedong proclaimed the establishment of the People's Republic of China (PRC) in Beiping, while some areas within the country still remained unconquered. As early as June 1949, the Communist party convened a preparatory committee to create the Chinese People's Political Consultative Conference as a multiparty and interclass organ to establish a base for the new China. During September in Beiping, the conference adopted an Organic Law and a Common Program, which became the administrative structure and philosophy for the Central People's Government of the People's Republic of China. Again, the northern capital of Beiping was renamed Beijing.

According to the Organic Law, the PRC was not a "Dictatorship of the Proletariat" along Soviet lines. Instead, it was a "Democratic Dictatorship" built on the basis of class alliance, with the CCP as the leader. The coexistence of four classes endowed the government with a "democratic" character, while its unbending and tough attitude toward the counterrevolutionaries gave it the attribute of a "dictatorship." The ruling principle of the new government was "Democratic Centralism," which applies to popular election at different levels of government. This concept meant that the process of election was "democratic," while obedience to higher authorities suggested "centralism."

The government structure comprised the Central People's Government Council (CPGC) at the highest level, which exercised executive, legislative, and judicial powers; the State Administrative Council headed by a premier (Zhou Enlai); and the provincial administrations including unique Great Administrative Areas, each with jurisdiction over several provinces. The CPGC members included the chairman (Mao), six vice-chairmen, and 56 others elected by the People's Political Consultative Council. Supreme power in the state rested with Mao, and this situation lasted until his death in 1976.

U.S. President Richard Nixon shares a toast with Premier Chou En-lai in 1972.

CHAPTER 15

MAO'S CHINA: THE FIRST DECADE

15.1 SOCIALIST TRANSFORMATION

On October 1, 1949, Mao Zedong solemnly proclaimed the founding of the People's Republic of China (PRC). After a period of economic recovery in the following three years (1950-1952), the basic realization of the socialist transformation of agriculture, the handicrafts industry, and capitalist industry and commerce was implemented from 1953 to 1956. While developing production, China gradually established socialist public ownership of the means of production. Mao meticulously divided his reform ideas into stages, and the first, dubbed the First Five-Year Plan (1953-1957), which was for the development of the national economy, was achieved ahead of schedule. China established and expanded basic industries necessary for full industrialization, producing airplanes, automobiles, heavy machinery, precision machinery, power-generating equipment, metallurgical and mining equipment, high-grade alloy steels and non-ferrous metals. The leading role of public ownership of the means of production had been defined, and the transition from new democracy to socialism had been realized.

Between 1953 and 1956, the annual average increase in the gross output value of industry was 19.6 percent and of agriculture 4.8 percent. During that period, more than 110 large industrial enterprises were completed, mostly in heavy industry. This laid the groundwork for Chinese socialist industrialization. By 1957, the value of industrial output of state-owned enterprises reached around 53 percent, and that of collectively owned ones reached 19 percent. The remaining industrial enterprises were in the category of either joint state/ private ownership or private ownership.

Planning in that period was relatively flexible; the scope for control was limited to minor parts of the state-owned enterprises, important materials, and projects. Indirect control of the cooperative, individual, private capitalist, and state capitalist economy was through proper economic policies, the pricing system, taxation, and the credit system. In the agriculture sector, the Agrarian Reform Law of the PRC was promulgated in June 1950. After land reform, the agricultural production system was changed in three stages: the mutual aid team, the elementary agricultural producers' cooperative, and the advanced agricultural producers' cooperative.

From 1957 to 1966, China began large-scale socialist construction. Overall, considerable achievements were made in the national economy during this decade in spite of some serious mistakes in economic construction. Fixed assets in industry grew four times in value, while national income increased by 58 percent in terms of comparable prices and by 34 percent in terms of per capita amount. From 1966 to 1976, the ten-year

Cultural Revolution brought China its biggest setback since 1949. In spite of this, China as a whole still had a relatively high rate of economic growth during that period. Grain output rose from 193 million tons in 1956 to 282.73 million tons in 1977. Also during this period, crude steel output rose from 4.45 million to 23.74 million tons, coal from 11 million to 93.6 million tons, chemical fertilizers from 0.133 million to 7.238 million tons, machine tools from 25,928 to 198,700 sets, and cotton cloth from 5.770 billion to 10.151 billion meters.

The aim of the ownership system of that period was to strengthen the state-owned economic system and supplant the collectively owned system. Private ownership had almost been abolished. In rural areas, the rural commune economy was established. In the commercial sector, the sales of state-owned enterprises reached over 90 percent during this period. The commodity circulation system suffered considerably.

The scope of mandatory planning in the coordination system increased after 1956, while during the period of the Great Leap Forward (1958-1960), planning control was decentralized to the provincial level. Because of the lack of effective macro-control, the economic system did not function efficiently. Central planning was once again emphasized in the adjustment period of 1963-1965, but because the planning system was again disrupted throughout the period of the Cultural Revolution, there were no improvements or modifications in the conception or practice of planning at that time.

15.2 THE SINO-SOVIET ALLIANCE

The People's Republic of China, born in the campaigns against imperialism, feudalism and bureaucratic capitalism, suffered imperialist hostility, blockade, and armed threat from the very beginning. At first, only some socialist countries headed by the Soviet Union and some neighboring countries supported China. Therefore, China entered an alliance with the Soviet Union, which gave great economic and technological assistance to China's economic construction in the 1950s.

Following the establishment of Sino-Soviet diplomatic relations, an important question calling for prompt solution in Sino-Soviet relations emerged: how to handle the 1945 Sino-Soviet Treaty of Friendship and Alliance signed by the Nationalist government and the Soviet Union so as to set forth anew the guiding principles and legal basis for the new Sino-Soviet relations in a changed situation. During his visit to the Soviet Union in the winter of 1949, Chairman Mao Zedong suggested to Stalin that a new treaty be signed by the two countries to replace the outdated Sino-Soviet Treaty. To this the Soviet side agreed. Subsequently, Premier Zhou Enlai led a Chinese government delegation to the Soviet Union for the negotiations. On February 14, 1950, the two sides signed the Sino-Soviet *Treaty of Friendship, Alliance and Mutual Assistance*, and other agreements. The foreign ministers of the two countries exchanged three notes, declaring null and void the old Sino-Soviet Treaty of Friendship and Alliance, and the other agreements that were signed by the Soviet Government and the Nationalist government of China on August 14, 1945.

The Sino-Soviet *Treaty of Friendship, Alliance and Mutual Assistance* of 1950 consisted of a preface and six articles, and remained in force for a term of 30 years. Its main contents were as follows: (1) The Two Contracting Parties strive to carry out jointly all necessary measures within their power to prevent a repetition of aggression and breach of the peace by Japan or any other State that might directly or indirectly join with Japan in acts of aggression. Should either be attacked by Japan and thus find itself in a state of war, the other Contracting Party shall immediately extend military and other assistance with all the means at its disposal; (2) Neither of the Contracting Parties shall enter into any alliance directed against the other Party, or participate in any coalition, action, or measure directed against the other Party; (3) The two contracting Parties shall undertake to consult together on all important international questions involving the common interests of the Soviet Union and China, with a view to strengthen peace and universal security; and (4) The two Contracting Parties shall undertake, in a spirit of friendship and cooperation, and in accordance with the principles of equal rights, mutual interests, mutual respect for State sovereignty and territorial integrity, and non-intervention in the domestic affairs of the other Party — this will be done in order to develop and strengthen the economic and cultural ties between the Soviet Union and China, to render each other all possible economic assistance, and to effect the necessary economic cooperation.

Under the historical circumstances of the time, the Sino-Soviet *Treaty of Friendship, Alliance and Mutual Assistance*, concluded between China and the Soviet Union, was of great significance in preserving the security of both sides, maintaining peace in East Asia and the world as a whole, strengthening friendship between the two peoples, and promoting the cause for socialist construction of the two countries.

But at the end of 1950s, contradictions and conflicts between the two countries became increasingly intensified. In addition to disputes concerning ideology, the main problem concerned the great-power chauvinism and hegemonism pursued by the Soviet Union. China refused its demands, which damaged China's sovereignty. In July 1960, the Soviet Union decided to unilaterally tear up economic and technological cooperation agreements between the two countries, and withdraw Soviet experts from China. Thus, the alliance was broken. After 1965, the Soviet Union deployed more than 1 million soldiers along the Sino-Soviet and Sino-Mongolian borders. The Chinese people rejected this great pressure with dauntless spirit. The confrontation lasted for more than 20 years, until early 1989, when leaders of the two countries met in Beijing and normalized relations.

15.3 THE GREAT LEAP FORWARD AND ITS AFTERMATH

In 1956-57, the Party undertook a campaign of ideological rectification known as the Anti-Rightist movement, designed to expose and isolate elements in the intellectual and cultural realms that were seen as undermining or resisting the transition to socialism. This led to public criticism and sometimes exile or other punishment of large numbers of academics and professionals, and led to increasing alienation between the Party and the educated strata in Chinese society. The anti-rightist drive was followed by a more militant approach toward economic development. In 1958, the CCP launched the Great Leap Forward Campaign under the new "General Line for Socialist Construction." The Great Leap Forward Campaign was aimed at accomplishing the economic and technical development of the country at a vastly faster pace and with greater results.

The shift to the left that the new "General Line" represented was brought on by a combination of domestic and external factors. Although the party leaders appeared to be generally satisfied with the accomplishments of the First Five-Year Plan, Mao and his fellow radicals believed that more could be achieved in the Second Five-Year Plan (1958-62) if the people could be ideologically aroused, and if domestic resources could be utilized more efficiently for the simultaneous development of industry and agriculture. These assumptions led the party to an intensified mobilization of the peasantry and mass organizations, stepped-up ideological guidance and indoctrination of technical experts, and increased efforts to build a more responsive political system. The last of these undertakings was to be accomplished through a new *xia-fang* (down to the countryside) movement, through which cadres inside and outside the party would be sent to factories, communes, mines, and public works projects for manual labor and firsthand familiarization with grass-roots conditions. Although evidence was sketchy, Mao's decision to embark on the Great Leap Forward Campaign was based in part on his uncertainty about the Soviet policy of economic, financial, and technical assistance to China. That policy, in Mao's view, not only fell far short of his expectations and needs but also made him wary of the political and economic dependence upon which China might find itself.

The Great Leap Forward Campaign centered on a new socio-economic and political system created in the countryside and in a few urban areas — the people's communes. By the fall of 1958, some 750,000 agricultural producers' cooperatives, now designated as production brigades, had been amalgamated into about 23,500 communes, each averaging 5,000 households, or the equivalent of 22,000 people. The individual commune was placed in control of all the means of production and was to operate as the primary accounting unit. It was subdivided into production brigades (generally coterminous with traditional villages) and production teams. Each commune was planned as a self-supporting community for agriculture and small-scale local industry, and was prepared to install schooling, marketing, administration, and local security (maintained by militia organizations). Organized along paramilitary and laborsaving lines, the commune had communal kitchens, mess halls, and nurseries.

In a way, the people's communes constituted a fundamental attack on the institution of the family, especially in a few model areas in which radical experiments in communal living — large dormitories in place of the traditional nuclear family housing — occurred. The system was also based on the assumption that it would release additional manpower for such major projects as irrigation works and hydroelectric dams, which were seen as integral parts of the plan for the simultaneous development of industry and agriculture.

The Great Leap Forward Campaign was an economic failure. In early 1959, amid signs of rising popular restlessness, the CCP admitted that the favorable production report for 1958 had been exaggerated. Among the Great Leap Forward Campaign's economic consequences were a drastic shortage of food (in which natural disasters also played a part); shortage of raw materials for industry; overproduction of poor-quality goods; deterioration of industrial plant through mismanagement; and exhaustion and demoralization of the peasantry, intellectuals, and party and government cadres at all levels. Throughout 1959, efforts to modify the administration of the communes got under way; these were intended partly to restore some material incentives to the production brigades and teams, partly to decentralize control, and partly to house families that had been reunited as household units.

Political fallout was feared by the leadership. The shortage of food resulted in a famine in some parts of the countryside. In April 1959, Mao, who bore the chief responsibility for the Great Leap Forward Campaign fiasco, stepped down from his position as chairman of the People's Republic. The National People's Congress elected Liu Shaoqi as Mao's successor, though Mao remained chairman of the CCP. Moreover, Mao's Great Leap Forward policy came under open criticism at a party conference at Lushan, Jiangxi Province. The attack was led by Defense Minister Peng Dehuai, who had become troubled by the potentially adverse effect Mao's policies would have on the modernization of the armed forces. Peng argued that "putting politics in command" was no substitute for economic laws and realistic economic policy; unnamed party leaders were also admonished for trying to "jump into communism in one step." After the Lushan showdown, Peng Dehuai, who allegedly had been encouraged by Soviet leader Nikita Khrushchev to oppose Mao, was deposed. Peng was replaced by Lin Biao, a radical and opportunist Maoist.

CHAPTER 16

CHINA IN CRISIS

16.1 THE GREAT PROLETARIAN CULTURAL REVOLUTION

Following the drastic plummeting of the national economy after the Great Leap Forward, more and more significant party members within the Chinese leadership began to question the precipitous course of Mao Zedong, who still ruled the country with a guerrilla mentality and favored class struggle and politics-in-command policies. In the year of 1959, all bad results appeared: indigenous production methods entailed an enormous waste of materials and a high cost of operation, while yielding low-quality products. Due to the failure of the communes and the aftermath of the Sino-Soviet split, the total GNP (Gross National Product) had dropped from US $95 billion in 1958, to US $92 billion in 1959, to US $89 billion in 1960, and to US $72 billion in 1961. All in all, the outcomes of the first years of the Great Leap and the communes were highly unsatisfactory, and there was great discontent among the people. Thus, some more pragmatic and less idealistic officials who exerted actual control over the daily operations of the party and the government decided to subtly block, divert, or modify the implementation of Mao's policies. Another reason for them to do so was because the pragmatists acquired great influence, while Mao retreated to the "second line" after the party reorganization in 1956. Through this reshuffle, Liu Shaoqi and Deng Xiaoping gradually came to the front stage of politics, appointed as first vice-chairman and party general secretary, respectively.

The Lushan Conference was followed by three years of poor harvest, bad weather, and a drop in agricultural and industrial production. Deeply touched by the misery of the people, Liu Shaoqi persuaded the Central committee in 1962 to adopt a domestic line of allowing the peasants to cultivate their own modest plots, operate small private handicraft enterprises, and sell their products at rural free markets. As a result, Liu began to attract a following and these people were known as Liuists. Mao was alarmed by the prospect of the return of capitalism and the rise of a new mandarin class. He was also concerned with the lack of revolutionary challenge among the youth. To obviate a revival of the old cultural tradition, Mao ordered a Socialist Education Movement in September 1962, commanding officials and intellectuals to be sent downward (*xia-fang*) to the countryside to learn from the masses. Having seen the resistance of the Liuists towards this new movement, Mao felt a challenge to his authority, and he was determined to fight back by giving them a thorough shakeup, reshuffling the power structure, re-establishing his supreme authority, and effecting an "irreversible transformation" of the people's thought and behavioral patterns. That was the astounding Cultural Revolution.

On November 10, 1965, an article entitled "Comment on the Newly Composed Historical Play 'Hai Rui Dismissed From Office'" — written by the editor-in-chief of the Shang-

117

hai branch of the *Liberation Army Daily*, Yao Wenyuan — launched what came to be known as the Great Proletarian Cultural Revolution or the Cultural Revolution. He attacked Wu Han, the deputy mayor of Beijing who had previously written a story about a mid-16th century official, Hai Rui, in which he scolded the Ming emperor for being arbitrary in his judgements. Yao accused Wu of likening Hai Rui to the dismissed Defense Minister Peng Dehuai, and the emperor to Mao. Actually, there were three famous intellectuals in Beijing openly engaged in criticizing the leadership: Wu Han, Deng Tuo, and Liao Mosha. It seemed that they may have been puppets of higher officials, namely the Beijing mayor Peng Zhen, and Liu Shaoqi. In the summer of 1965, Mao flew to Shanghai to lead a counteroffensive: he branded Liu and Peng as revisionists just as Khrushchev had been perceived in Russia, won military support from Lin Biao by promoting him to the second-ranking member in the CCP hierarchy, and called for the creation of the Red Guards — a group of "revolutionary youth" acting as the vanguard of the Cultural Revolution and the most loyal to Mao. On August 5, Mao wrote the first wall poster: "Bomb the (Liu-Deng) Headquarters!"

The Red Guards proved to be more a source of turmoil than revolutionary successors. They wrote big-character wall posters, ransacked private property, rampaged through cities, attacked those with modern attire and haircuts, and humiliated foreign diplomats. Soon things ran out of control, and Mao had to call in the army to help restabilize society. As the commander of the PLA, Lin Biao was ambitious, and further deepened his influence in the government, which paved the way for conspiracy.

16.2 THE LIN BIAO AFFAIR (1971)

Traditionally, the Chinese Communist army refrained from political participation, and strictly obeyed the civilian government. However, after Lin Biao rose to second place at the Ninth Party Congress, this rule was changed. The PLA came to occupy important positions in the political structure, and the military won a majority of seats on the Central Committee, the Politburo, and in provincial delegations. The situation was even enhanced during the Cultural Revolution, when the military quickly filled the vacuum created by the decimation of the party under Mao's call in January 1967. Of the ten marshals of the PLA, Lin Biao was among the graduates of the fourth class of Whampoa Military Academy, and had won many famous battles in the Civil War (1945-1949). After he replaced Peng Dehuai, Lin's influence in the army came to its peak.

While consolidating his control of the military, Lin Biao was equally concerned with establishing his image as a theorist and successor to the Thought of Mao. With the publication in September 1965 of his treatise "Long Live the Victory of the People's War," Lin soared beyond his command of the military to become China's second highest leader. However, while singing continuous praise of Mao, Lin Biao was steadily expanding his control of the armed forces, the party, the government, and the provinces. There were two things that stood in his way: specifically, his position seemed to violate the Maoist dictum that "the party commands the gun, and the gun will never be allowed to command the party." The other was his paranoia. The history of Chinese Communism is full of the unexpected, and only time could tell what was in Mao's mind. Actually, as early as 1966, Mao already became alarmed about Lin's interest in seizing power. Right after the Ninth Party Congress, Mao began to shift his position and entrust

Zhou Enlai to rebuild a civilian party. There is also evidence that in autumn 1968, differences of opinion between Mao and Lin already developed over the purge of party members. Mao thought the army had been too zealous and violent in doing so.

In March 1970, Mao decided to abolish the state chairmanship, which would preclude Lin's seizure of the position. Sensing the possibility of losing influence, Lin Biao was eager to do anything to prevent that event from happening. On the second Plenum of the Ninth Central Committee held at Lushan in August 1970, the Mao-Zhou group for the first time faced an open challenge by its antagonists, namely from Lin Biao and Chen Boda, who were buttressed by an array of military figures. From August 23 to mid-day August 25, a surprise attack was carried out and then failed. This was branded later in 1973 as the first of two abortive attempts to kill Mao.

After the second Lushan Conference, Lin gradually began to feel that a military coup was the only solution. Mao started a counterattack by assaulting Chen Boda and Lin's other followers first. Lin put his son, Lin Liguo, an Air force general, in charge of planning a coup. Between March 22-24, 1971, a small group of conspirators secretly gathered in Shanghai, and prepared the "5-7-1 Engineering Outline," the meaning of which is similar to an "armed uprising." The plan was said to have had the support of Moscow. To avoid a military rebellion, Mao flew to Nanjing and Guangzhou to command the regional generals to relinquish their political role, to ensure that they were at last neutralized. Having been betrayed by one of his co-conspirators, Li Weixin, deputy secretary of the Political Department of the Fourth Air Force, Lin hurriedly fled the country. When Mao grounded all planes, Lin's son managed to locate a Trident Jet No. 256, which lacked adequate fuel, a navigator, or even a radio operator. All the Lin family boarded and took off for Mongolia in the direction of the Soviet Union. The plane attempted a forced landing in order to refuel at an airstrip near Under Khan in Outer Mongolia, but its wings hit the ground and all were said to have perished in the crash on September 13, 1971. Later the Lin Biao Affair was described by Mao as one of the most serious struggles within the party in its fifty-year history.

16.3 THE GANG OF FOUR IN POWER AND DEATH OF MAO (1976)

During the Cultural Revolution, Mao Zedong's wife Jiang Qing developed a strong interest in politics, and gradually engaged herself in the power struggles under Mao's patronage. It was said that Mao had opened a way to propel his wife into the forefront of national politics through launching the Cultural Revolution, thereby positioning her for an ultimate bid for the succession.

Since the early 1960s, Jiang Qing had been active in reforming the arts and produced eight "model operas." She then took over the media as a prelude to winning control of the national culture and the people's minds, with an intention of utilizing propaganda as the basis of her personal power and authority. She was a major facilitator of the Cultural Revolution. In 1965, she accompanied Mao to Shanghai and jointly directed Yao Wenyuan to fire the first shot of the Cultural Revolution. On November 22, 1966, when a seventeen-member Central Cultural Revolutionary Committee was formed, Jiang Qing was made the first vice-chairwoman. She and her three other associates, Yao Wenyuan, Zhang Chunqiao, and Wang Hongwen, were later known as the Gang of Four.

During the upheavals, the Cultural Revolutionary Group under Jiang Qing and her followers pursued a ruthless purge of party high cadres. Vowing to uphold the Thought of Mao, they were determined to rub out bourgeois influences and revisionist tendencies, and to eliminate all the old thought, culture, customs, and habits. Under this pretense, a lot of precious cultural heritage was destroyed, and the lives of millions of people were thrown into great disturbance.

After the fall of Lin Biao, at the Tenth Party Congress in August 1973, the Gang of Four made an intense bid for power. Jiang Qing and Yao Wenyuan were elected to the Politburo, and Zhang Chunqiao to its Standing Committee. Wang Hongwen, a 37-year-old protégé of Jiang Qing, was made the second vice-chairman of the party. At the Congress, Wang spoke for the radical Cultural Revolutionary Group, announcing that the smashing of bourgeois groups headed by Liu Shaoqi and Lin Biao was the accomplishment of the Great Proletarian Cultural Revolution. Thus, he turned the Cultural Revolution into an ongoing process, extending from the mid-1960s to the future. After the death of Zhou Enlai on January 8, 1976, the struggle for the premiership became fierce. The Gang of Four tried to replace the pragmatist Deng Xiaoping, the chosen successor of Zhou, with the radical candidate Zhang Chunqiao. However, Zhang was not favored by many senior party cadres. In his waning health, Mao's loyalty was caught between his wife and the old cadres. Finally Mao chose a neutral person, Hua Guofeng, a top security official from his home of Hunan, who was neither a pragmatist nor a radical.

Shortly after Hua's appointment, between March 29 and April 4, many people went to Tiananmen Square to pay tribute to Premier Zhou during the Qingming Festival, a traditional commemoration of the dead. Angry about the Gang of Four, they showed support for Zhou and Deng, while indirectly criticizing Mao as arbitrary and incompetent. This was known as the Tiananmen Square Incident of 1976. Deng Xiaoping was accused of orchestrating these protests and was immediately purged from his leadership positions. On September 9, 1976, Mao Zedong, who had been holding power until the last day of his life, passed away after suffering for many years from Parkinson's disease. Losing their protector, the political life of Jiang Qing and the Gang of Four soon came to an end.

CHAPTER 17

CHINA WITHOUT MAO

17.1   THE SMASHING OF THE GANG OF FOUR

The death of one of China's most powerful leaders, Mao Zedong, created great strife throughout China in 1976. The question of by whom he would be succeeded became a national concern. An intense power struggle arose as his wife, Jiang Qing, desired to succeed him as chairman. Jiang Qing and her three associates, who came to be known collectively as the Gang of Four, conspired to seize power. Unfortunately, their aspirations were blocked by Hua Guofeng. As the first vice-chairman of the party, premier of the State Council, and Mao's entrusted apprentice, Hua had a first claim to succession.

Although Jiang Qing's power and influence weakened as a result of her husband's death, she continued to control the media and the urban militia in key places such as Shanghai, Beijing, Tianjin, Shenyang, and Guangzhou. She and her colleagues planned for a rebellion by preparing a National General

124

Militia Headquarters to challenge the Military Commission in Beijing. The Gang of Four also received additional military support from Mao's nephew, Mao Yuanxin, political commissar of the Shenyang Military Region. He organized a task force in preparation for a march on Beijing to support the plan for a rebellion. In spite of this support, the Jiang Qing faction remained weak militarily due to the militia's lack of firepower and good commanders. Jiang Qing then decided to recruit two militarily powerful Politburo members, General Chen Xilian and Su Zhenhua. Unfortunately, both men informed Hua of Jiang's plans. Chen's and Su's weakness in the political arena empowered senior party cadres and military leaders, who had once been powerless against them, to make plans that would prevent the two men from seizing power. They entrusted Ye Jianying, minister of defense, with the task of developing a friendship with Hua and promising him their support as Mao's successor. Other anti-Gang of Four operations were also secretly under way. Deng Xiaoping, dismissed and hunted by the Gang of Four, had fled to Guangzhou under the protection of Ye Jianying and Xu Shiyou. In collaboration with other political leaders, these three secretly attended a meeting that was aimed at fighting the Gang of Four by forming an alliance with the Fuzhou and Nanjing Military Regions. They planned to establish a rival Central Committee to oppose Jiang Qing, if she ever gained power.

Meanwhile, the Gang of Four plotted to assassinate Politburo members including Hua and Ye. Hua and Ye became allies and, along with Wang Dongxing, commander of Mao's bodyguard, they planned to rebel against the Gang of Four by securing Shanghai. General Xu Shiyou of the Guangzhou Military Region was enlisted to obtain the cooperation of the Shanghai garrison commander, and win control of this key city before the urban militia could act.

Jiang Qing had been developing plans for seizing power since her husband's death. She used her strong influence over the media to play up a chairman's "deathbed adjuration." She tampered with Mao's documents, manipulating Chinese characters to state that Mao wished for individuals to support Jiang Qing and help her "carry the Red Banner." Jiang Qing argued that she intended to be Mao's successor. Under Jiang's control, these statements were published in Chinese newspapers. Hua became enraged as he read the false statements. He believed that succession should be decided according to past principles, namely that the first vice-chairman of the party should succeed the deceased chairman until the next session of the Central Committee elected a new chairman.

Hua pointed out the "wrong propaganda policy" at a Politburo meeting. Jiang Qing responded by saying that Hua was incompetent to lead the party and demanded that she be made chairwoman of the Central Committee. Hua replied by saying that he was not only competent but knew how to "solve problems," indirectly referring to the removal of the Four from power.

The Gang of Four prepared to achieve victory. It secretly set October 6, 1976, as the date of its rebellion. Meanwhile, the anti-Gang of Four forces were getting ready to strike. An article by Liang Xiao in the *Guangming Daily* was regarded as a "mobilization order." It stated that Mao's adjuration would "forever be the guide for continuous advance and the guarantee of victory to the members of the Chinese Communist Party . . . All chieftains of the revisionist line who attempt to tamper with this principle laid down necessarily have to tamper with Marxist-Leninist-Mao Zedong Thought." It warned that no "revisionist chieftain" would dare to challenge Mao's adjuration. On October 5, 1976, a secret meeting involving Hua, Ye, Wang, Beijing Garrison Commander Chen Xilian, and Vice-Premier Li

Xianian was held in the headquarters of the commander of the People's Liberation Army. The group decided that it had to act quickly before the Gang of Four began its rebellion. It planned to safeguard Beijing, arrest the Four, guard the Great Wall against possible attack from Shenyang, and transfer a regiment to Beijing in order to watch over the 38th regiment. The Gang of Four and its associates were arrested on October 6, 1976. Hua, Wang, and Ye delivered reports containing charges against the Gang of Four. The grateful Politburo named Hua chairman of the party Central Committee and chairman of the Military Commission, and put him in charge of editing the fifth volume of the *Selected Works of Mao Zedong*. On October 24, 1976, a million soldiers and civilians held a victory rally at Tiananmen Square to celebrate the smashing of the Gang of Four. Hua was hailed a "worthy leader" of the party. The Third Plenary Session of the Tenth Central Committee described the smashing of the Gang of Four as the eleventh major struggle in the history of the party.

On December 10, 1976, the Central Committee issued a document entitled "Evidence of Crimes of the Anti-Party Clique of Wang Hongwen, Zhang Chunqiao, Jiang Qing, and Yao Wenyuan." The Four were charged with attempted "usurpation of the Party and seizure of power," the crime of adulterating the line laid down by Mao, crimes against Hua Guofeng after he became acting Premier and premier-first-vice chairman, and attacking the party during Mao's illness and after his death. The Gang of Four was permanently expelled from the party, removed from all official posts, and branded as conspiratorial, ultra-rightist, counterrevolutionary, and representative of the Guomindang.

17.2 THE REHABILITATION OF DENG XIAOPING

With the death of Mao and the downfall of the Gang of Four, China entered a new period of change. China's priorities were thoroughly reorganized. The government and its people wanted normalcy, stability, and modernization. It was time for a new beginning.

Chairman Hua Guofeng was challenged with three issues: his authority as Mao's successor, the rehabilitation of Deng Xiaoping, and the task of modernization. Many thought that Hua's succession was unconstitutional because it reflected Mao's personal view rather than the will of the party. Although Hua believed that he was a legitimate candidate as Mao's successor, he agreed to the reinstatement of Deng. As a result of mediation by Marshal Ye and Vice-Premier Li Xiannian, Hua agreed to rehabilitate Deng, and to revise the five-year economic plan to accelerate the Four Modernizations in agriculture, industry, science and technology, and national defense, all of which were Deng's main policies.

Deng's many supporters in the party and the army planned an extensive campaign demanding his rehabilitation. There were demonstrations and wall posters calling for his return to office. The Politburo cleared Deng of involvement in the Tiananmen Square Incident of April 1976. Hua polled the Central Committee members to examine their views on the Deng case. The Politburo overwhelmingly agreed to restore Deng to his former position provided that he admit to his past mistakes.

In the Third Plenum of the Tenth Central Committee meeting, three resolutions were passed to confirm earlier Politburo decisions. The first resolution was the approval of Hua as chairman of the party and of the Military Commission. The second resolution was the acceptance of Hua's recommendation that Deng be restored to his former positions including Politburo Standing Committee member, and vice-chairman of the Central Committee. The last resolution condemned the antiparty activities of the Gang of Four. With the Gang of Four and its chief supporters removed, reorganization within the party occurred. The Politburo power structure fell into three groups: Hua and Deng each had nine supporters, and Ye had five supporters. None of the three commanded a majority, and Ye held the balance within the group. Despite the presence of emerging power struggles, the Congress called for unity, discipline, stability, and cooperation. A Disciplinary Committee was established to monitor the conduct of all party members. This post-Gang of Four period reflected euphoric feelings toward ambition and progress. Hua called for unity, modernization, better international relations, a 10 percent industrial growth rate, and a 4 to 5 percent annual increase in agricultural production. These targets were thought to be overly ambitious, but "nothing seemed impossible."

17.3 THE POLITICAL COALITION AND RISE OF DENG

Despite the unity represented in the three-way partnership of Hua, Ye, and Deng, tension began to escalate. Although Hua treated Deng with respect, Deng was subtly condescending towards Hua. Deng's strategy for political control created conflict with Hua. Deng increased his power base by rehabilitating those who had suffered under Mao and the Gang of Four. He took a strong stand against leaders associated with the Cultural Revolution and the Gang of Four, which included Hua. Deng weakened Hua's power by attacking his associates. He also developed able, young followers, and placed them in positions that would direct them to achieve his economic policies. Deng also shattered his former opponents' power base

129

by combating the innate supremacy of "Mao Thought." As a result, the post-Gang of Four government confronted the question of Mao's leadership, and his responsibility for the Cultural Revolution and China's troubles.

The Fifth National People's Congress (NPC) met again from June 18 to July 1, 1979, to discuss and ratify earlier decisions reached by the party Central Committee in December 1978. The ratifications involved the following: establishing the dominance of agriculture and its development; shifting the focus of state and party work to socialist construction, while revising targets for the Four Modernizations; enacting a legal system for the protection and development of democracy; and approving personnel changes in government.

Hua and Deng reached an implied understanding. Hua would support Deng's personnel changes and economic policies, while Deng would allow Hua to issue a critical review of Mao's role in the Cultural Revolution. This review would be embarrassing and injurious to Hua, who had strongly supported Mao. Meanwhile, the NPC continued to call for stability, unity, modernization, reform of the legal system, and greater democracy, all of which had been unrealized ambitions during Mao's rule of turmoil, factional conflicts, and poor economic planning. The prospect of an improving economy, more realistic modernization goals, and a better-protected democracy brought national unity and stability. Chairman Hua was allowed to retain his premiership for the moment. He was helped by his support for the cause of farmers and the Four Modernizations. The NPC, however, showed that Deng was stronger in the development of economic policy and in enhancing his power base. Despite their political rivalry, the Hua-Deng leadership was committed to national reconstruction through economic development, modernization, and stability.

The Fifth Plenum of the Eleventh Central Committee marked the end of the transitional period from Mao's death to the rise of Deng as the most powerful figure in Chinese politics. The party rejected Mao's "politics in command" for Deng's "economics in command." The party hoped to turn China into an advanced nation by the year 2040, and called for the support of its people.

CHAPTER 18

CHINA'S OPEN DOOR

18.1 THE NEW ORDER UNDER DENG XIAOPING

The Fifth Plenum of the Eleventh Central Committee, February 23-29, 1980, confirmed the rise of Deng Xiaoping as the most powerful figure in Chinese politics. Deng's "economics in command" became the guiding principle. Any dissent from the central government's new policies and beliefs was not tolerated. Deng did not want the Chinese people to spin out of control with their newfound freedoms, and thus what resulted was a "restrained democracy." This trend towards limiting government dissent was not limited to Democracy Wall activists, whose activities were suppressed late in 1979. Politburo members who were not enthusiastic towards Deng and his policies were immediately dismissed. Deng had long urged separating party and government functions as well as ending lifelong appointments for cadres. His reorganization plan was approved by the Fifth National People's Congress at its Third Plenum (August 29-Sept 10, 1980). This insured an orderly transfer of power to a collective leadership of relatively young pragmatists committed to modernization regardless of the fate of Deng and other aging leaders. As a demonstration of good faith, Deng and six other Vice-Premiers resigned. The National People's Congress was only concerned with government appointments. For the first time an orderly transfer of power seemed to have been arranged while the previous incumbents were still healthy, which created a precedent for future leaders.

18.2 THE OPEN DOOR POLICY AND FOUR MODERNIZATIONS

OPEN DOOR POLICY

In the first decade of the People's Republic (1949-1959), China maintained diplomatic and commercial relations only with the Soviet Union and Eastern European states. With the Sino-Soviet split in 1959, China was becoming more isolated. It was not until 1972, with U.S. President Richard Nixon's visit to China, that limited commercial relations began to be constructed with the outside world. In December of 1978, the CCP reversed the Maoist policy of seclusion and adopted the Open Door Policy. Deng realized that in order for China to modernize, it must import foreign science, technology, capital, and management skills. Japan, Hong Kong, West Germany, and the U.S. quickly became China's largest trading partners. Japan enjoyed a particularly special relationship due to its geographical proximity and degree of cultural affinity. Japan's prior economic success enabled it to offer China loans, grants, and preferential tariffs. Hong Kong also maintained importance in its link between China and the international community.

During the 1980s, China diversified its exports, raised quality levels, devalued the Chinese *yuan*, and eagerly adapted to international business practices to improve its competitive edge. In purchasing, it adhered to three criteria: good prices, good quality, and financing arrangements. China steadily built up its foreign currency reserves, and in 1981 it crossed the line from being a debtor nation to being a creditor nation. Chinese foreign trade grew annually by 20 percent in imports, and 10 to 15 percent in exports. The only sector that was lacking was foreign investment, for which the Chinese took the following measures to improve: (1) they opened four Special Economic Zones (SEZs) in 1979; (2) opened fourteen coastal cities to foreign investment in 1984; (3) hosted international conferences to advertise projects needing foreign assistance; (4) granted permission to local authorities to arrange for foreign investments without central government approval; (5) passed laws and regulations on taxation, liability, and other intellectual property rights' issues; and (6) clarified arbitration procedures, labor compensation, and repatriation of foreign profit from China. Despite these efforts, foreigners still found the Chinese investment environment to be unstable and unprofitable. However, simultaneous reforms in other sectors continued to provide prosperity and increased living standards in the countryside as well as the cities.

FOUR MODERNIZATIONS

The Four Modernizations in the sectors of agriculture, industry, science and technology, and national defense were designed to turn China into a leading modern state by the year 2040. However, the original ten-year plan was more of a wish than an economic blueprint. In the first year of the program, which was written into the party constitution on August 18, 1977, some 100,000 construction projects were launched by the government with costs totaling over US $40 billion.

This unsupportable zealous spending was quickly curbed, and henceforth only projects that could be completed quickly and earn foreign exchange were encouraged. The transportation and energy sectors remained major obstacles in the modernization plan, and the unexpected high cost of China's war with Vietnam in 1979 took its toll. Finally, in June of 1979, at the Fifth National People's Congress, government leaders announced a three-year period (1979-81) for the "adjustment, reconstruction, consolidation, and improvement" of the national economy. The immediate effect was the halting of 348 important heavy industrial projects, and 4,500 smaller ones.

Industrial Sector: The Ten-Year Plan, unveiled at the Fifth National People's Congress in February 1978 called for the investment in capital construction industry over the following decade to equal or surpass that of the combined previous 28 years. This was estimated to be an investment of US $40 billion, with an annual rate of industrial growth at 10 percent. The completion of 120 major projects was mandated, including 10 iron and steel complexes, 6 oil and gas fields, 30 power stations, 8 coal mines, 9 non-ferrous metal complexes, 7 major trunk railways, and 5 key harbors. It was hoped that the output in each major sector would approach, equal, or outstrip that of the most developed capitalist countries.

Agricultural Sector: This sector was seen as the foundation of the Chinese economy, and as such, the most important of all the modernizations. In 1977, the average grain per capita levels equaled that of those in 1955, reflecting heavy population increases and greater extraction of surplus for investment in the industrial sector. The Ten-Year Plan called for maximizing farm production through the mechanization of chemical fertilizers. The goals were to increase the gross agricultural product by 4 to 5 percent annually, increase food output to 400 million tons by 1985, expand water works, mechanize

85 percent of farming tasks, and establish 12 commodity and food base areas throughout the nation. The utilization of material incentive policies led to more pay for more work, and less pay for less work.

Scientific Modernization: At the National Science Conference in March 1978, Vice-Premier Fang Yi presented the "Draft Outline National Plan" for the development of science. The four aspects of the draft were as follows: (1) the attainment of the 1970 scientific levels of advanced nations; (2) the increase of professional scientific researchers to 800,000; (3) the development of up-to-date centers for science experiments; and (4) the completion of a nationwide system of scientific and technological research. There were 108 projects in 27 fields that were marked as key projects. It was hoped that through these advancements China would be only 10 years behind the developed nations by 1985.

Military Modernization: At the time of the introduction of the Four Modernizations, China had the largest armed force in the world, which consisted of over four million soldiers. However, it lacked advanced military technology, and Mao's previous principle of "spirit over weapons" had hindered the development of military ideas. Furthermore, the Chinese leaders were also hindered by the extreme cost of updating the military, but nevertheless spent US $32.8 billion in 1976 and US $35 billion in 1978. This was approximately 7 to 10 percent of China's GNP, and perhaps one of the highest rates of military expenditure in the world. With the expensive purchase of state-of-the-art weaponry and technology, it took the Chinese another 5 to 10 years to integrate the new products into their structures. Thus, they modernized the military, but still remained about 15 years behind that of the advanced nations.

18.3 BUILDING SOCIALISM WITH CHINESE CHARACTERISTICS

Deng Xiaoping knew that for any transformation to be successful, socialist construction in China must have Chinese characteristics, and that Marxism-Leninism must be integrated with Chinese realities. Deng did not have a specific plan in mind, but gradually determined a vision of what China's future should entail. Since 80 percent of the Chinese people lived in the countryside, invigorating the rural economy and raising farmers' incomes became the first order of business. The Open Door Policy was necessary for China to advance, since China's previous years of isolation had led to years of ignorance and backwardness. According to Deng, the mainstays of the Chinese economy would remain socialist, in that China would maintain the principle of state ownership of the main factors of production. Many CCP leaders worried that China's open door would lead to a capitalist revival. However, Deng did not believe that an influx of foreign capital would undermine socialist economic foundations since joint ventures with foreigners would be at least 50 percent Chinese. He also did not believe that a per capita annual GNP of several thousand dollars would lead to the rise of a new capitalist class.

Deng's strategy of "one step at a time, watch out and keep the momentum going," became the guiding principle of all his reforms. In the agricultural sector, the party adopted the use of greater material incentives, and loosened control mechanisms that had previously constrained growth in the rural sector. Under this strategy, the Responsibility System was created and placed into action in 1979. In this system, land ownership remained public, but each household received a plot for cultivation and negotiated a contract with the commune production team or economic cooperative. The contract specified quantities of crops to be planted and the quota of output to be handed to the production team as payment for the use of the land. Each household had full control of its labor resources and could either keep or sell the products that exceeded the quota. As a result of this system, yield and productivity rose sharply. A new type of township-collective-household rural structure emerged which assumed some of the former functions of the commune.

The industrial reform was a bit more complicated, and a bit less successful. The reform of any part of industry would disrupt the balance in the interlocking network of planning, management, production, marketing, and pricing, and thus reform was conducted in two phases. The first phase (1978-84) attempted to rekindle work enthusiasm, unleash the full potential of the workers, raise living standards, and inaugurate the use of material incentives. The Industrial Responsibility System emerged in this first phase, under which a state-owned enterprise (SOE) signed a profit-and-loss contract with its supervisory body, agreeing to remit a quota of profit to the state, while retaining a share of the remaining profits. By 1980, some 6,600 SOEs had come under this system. Industrial enterprises were made responsible for all their economic decisions, and thus the state lost control over local investments. The first phase was characterized by planning through guidance, not central planning and directives.

The second phase began October 20, 1984, with the passing of the new "Resolution on the Reform of the Economic System." This resolution was an optimistic statement of intent and principles for the guidance of 44 million party members. It further loosened government control over enterprises, and emphasized that public ownership need not be equated with direct state control: ownership and management were two separate functions. Private enterprises were now considered desirable, and the leasing or contracting of small and medium state enterprises to private parties was encouraged. This greatly increased the level of capital investment, but was unsustainable and created shortages of construction materials, waste, confusion, and inflation.

Finally, in January 1986, a retrenchment policy was issued to help save the economy from spiraling out of control. This policy highlighted four key concepts: (1) the consolidation of gains and solidification of reforms; (2) the digestion of changes and price reforms to tackle reform problem areas; (3) the supplementation and amendment of the problems of the reforms; and (4) the improvement of macroeconomic controls to achieve better balance between supply and demand. This did not stop the momentum of economic expansion, and growth was uneven between each sector.

Unknown protester blocks tanks in Tiananmen Square in 1989. Hundreds perished after the government repressed student-led pro-democracy demonstrations.

CHAPTER 19

REFORMS AND CRISES IN DENG'S CHINA

19.1 CHINA'S FOREIGN RELATIONS

After Deng Xiaoping consolidated his hold on power and ushered in the Four Modernizations, Chinese foreign policy became more pragmatic. The focus now shifted to turning China into a leading modern state by the year 2040.

Since the 1980s, Chinese officials have repeatedly emphasized the importance of economic development while underlining the danger posed by looming U.S. hegemony. The Chinese view is that in the 21st century, national power will derive primarily from economic, scientific, and technological prowess. Since the late 1980s, Beijing's leaders, especially those who have taken over national policy in the wake of Deng Xiaoping's enfeeblement, have set goals that are contrary to American interests. Driven by nationalist sentiment, a yearning to redeem the humiliations of the past, and the simple urge for international power, China is seeking to replace the United States as the dominant power in Asia. In the 1980s, many countries in Asia, Africa, Latin America, and Oceania established diplomatic relations with China. Since the beginning of the 1990s, China has established diplomatic relations with even more countries, such as Israel, the Republic of Korea and South Africa, as well as with the newly independent republics that emerged from the former Soviet Union. By mid-2002, 165 countries had established diplomatic relations with China.

For ideological as well as economic reasons, the Chinese have preferred to align themselves rhetorically with the poorer countries of the Third World and to distance themselves from the two superpowers. Despite China's technological achievements, it essentially remains a geographically large, developing country in need of economic assistance. And as a socialist country with a historical tradition of cultural superiority in the region, its periods of entente with the Soviet Union and the United States have often broken down. Yet, since the late 1980s, China's relations with both the United States and the Soviet Union have substantially improved.

Within the Pacific region, China is potentially a major economic and political force. Its relations with Japan, Korea, and its Southeast Asian neighbors — Vietnam, Cambodia, Laos, Malaysia, Thailand, Indonesia, Singapore, and the Philippines — will be determined by how these countries perceive China's power will be used. By the late 1980s, Japan had become China's primary trading partner and source of foreign investment. The Chinese remain sensitive to Japanese atrocities committed in their homeland during World War II, but the two countries also share a long history of cultural interchange.

After decades of strained relations, trade and cultural and educational exchanges between the United States and China are increasing. Although both countries agree that Taiwan is part of China, the United States has long supported the government of Taiwan and insists that reunification with the mainland should be achieved by peaceful means; China maintains that this is an internal matter to be settled amongst its own people, and protests the ever-present U.S. commitment to prevent a military attack on Taiwan by the Communists. Having experienced foreign encroachment and mediation in their internal affairs from the mid-19th to the mid-20th centuries, the Chinese remain sensitive to any perceived challenges to their national sovereignty.

In foreign affairs, China and Britain reached an agreement on the future of Hong Kong in 1984, and an accord between Portugal and China on Macao was reached in 1987. Improved relations with the Soviet Union were symbolized by a 1989 Sino-Soviet summit. After the 1989 crackdown on the pro-democracy movement, China nevertheless began to emerge from international isolation. Relations with the Soviet Union, however, were strained by the 1991 collapse of the Communist party there. At home, the deadlock between hard-liners and reformers within the CCP continued.

19.2 PRO-DEMOCRACY MOVEMENT

Economic reforms since the 1980s have led to disagreement among those who favor the "open-door" policy of contact and economic exchange with the West and those who fear the "spiritual pollution" and "bourgeois liberalization" of social and economic values that have accompanied economic exchange with the West. Just as in the late 19th century, three positions can be discerned among the Chinese leaders: (1) a "neo-traditional" interpretation of Marxism that contains many traditional Chinese values (deference to seniors, paternalistic government, economic self-sufficiency, a Chinese-centered rather than cosmopolitan culture); (2) complete Westernization, including the abandonment of socialism and Marxism (since it is illegal to voice these ideas openly, it is difficult to gauge their strength), a position held mainly by younger people and reformers; and (3) adoption of Western technology and managerial methods, while attempting to keep these elements distinct from the culture. The idea of "Chinese-style socialism" represents this desire to adopt all that is useful from the West while still retaining a distinctive, and indeed superior, Chinese cultural identity.

From the mid-1980s onward, under the primary influence of Deng Xiaoping, a certain amount of economic and political liberalization occurred. Economic reforms were initiated to increase incentives, promote economic relations with non-Communist nations, and reduce what was seen as rigid economic centralization. Intellectuals were encouraged to be more outspoken and to share in a new spirit of what was called "democratization." At the same time, party leaders in 1986 warned that modernization must not be used as an excuse to introduce "bourgeois philosophies and social doctrines."

Late in 1986, student groups in various parts of China began to engage in peaceful demonstrations aimed at encouraging more student participation in local government, a greater degree of democracy, and better living conditions. In December, large student demonstrations occurred in Shanghai, Beijing, and other cities. On January 16, 1987, Hu Yaobang, general secretary of the Chinese Communist Party who had been supporting greater liberalization, resigned from office, saying that he had made major mistakes and would take responsibility for them. While Hu's resignation was seen as a blow to the forces of political and economic change, he remained a symbol of increasing public sentiment in favor of more democracy.

144

In 1989, Soviet leader Mikhail Gorbachev introduced the world to *glasnost* (openness) and *perestroika* (restructuring). The utter collapse of Communism in Eastern Europe began with the disintegration of the Soviet Union, and the rise of both nationalistic and democratic movements on a broad scale. It marked the end of the Cold War and the arms race. And in the spring of 1989, a vibrant pro-democracy movement started in China.

Hu Yaobang's death, on April 15, 1989, sparked widespread public rallies in favor of broad social change in Beijing, Shanghai, and other cities. Tens of thousands of students and other categories of the population defied a ban on public gatherings, and led a demonstration in May in Beijing's central Tiananmen Square, and in front of the nearby headquarters of the CCP. Seeing that simply demonstrating would not achieve the desired results, many of the participants began to organize hunger strikes, drawing further outside attention to the rallies. After a lengthy period of apparent indecision by the party leadership, troops were sent into the square on June 3-4; hundreds of demonstrators perished and the crackdown resulted in widespread arrests. Following the repression in Beijing, Shanghai, and other cities, Deng Xiaoping appeared to be even more firmly in control, assisted by Li Peng, the premier. Zhao Ziyang, who was discredited by his efforts to reach an accommodation with the pro-democracy demonstrators, was dismissed from all of his posts. Jiang Zemin, Communist party chief in Shanghai, replaced Zhao as party general secretary in June 1989.

19.3 THE OTHER CHINA: TAIWAN IN OPPOSITION

When the Republican government moved to Taipei in 1949, the economy of Taiwan was still trying to recover from the heavy Allied bombing that had occurred during the war. In the initial years, two factors stabilized the situation and laid the foundations for a future economic takeoff: aid from the U.S., and a land reform program. From 1951 to 1965, large amounts of economic aid came from the U.S. as part of its Cold War efforts to preserve this valuable ally in Asia. Much of the aid was used in the agricultural sector. Advisors and programs that sent Taiwanese abroad for education were directed at rebuilding the economy. The highly successful land reform program, which was completed in 1953, reduced land rents, distributed public land, and purchased and resold land from large landlords. Farmers were supplied with fertilizer, seeds, pesticides, expert advice, and credit. By 1959, 90 percent of exports was agriculture or food related. Increased production and higher income resulted in low inflation and capital accumulation, since importing food was unnecessary.

After land reform policies and economic assistance had laid a solid foundation for the economy, two policies of the 1950s and 1960s led to Tawain's remarkable takeoff during the 1970s. The first was an "import substitution policy" aimed at making Taiwan self-sufficient by producing inexpensive consumer goods, processing imported raw materials, and restricting other imports. When far-sighted government planners realized the economic bottleneck posed by the narrow base of Taiwan's domestic economy, a second policy of "export promotion" was adopted in the late 1950s and continued throughout the 1960s. Using Japan as a model and employing U.S. advice, the resource-poor, labor-rich island began to expand light manufacturing. Export processing zones, free of bureaucratic red-tape and motivated by special tax incentives, were set up to attract overseas investment. Soon, Taiwan secured an international reputation as an exporter to the world.

Between 1962 and 1985, Taiwan's economy witnessed the most rapid growth in its history: an average annual rate of nearly 10 percent, over twice the average economic growth rate of industrialized countries during this period. Equitable distribution of income was a major objective in the government's economic planning. A new and highly significant economic trend beginning in the 1980s was the rise of investment by the Taiwan business community on the Chinese mainland. After the Emergency Decree was lifted in 1987, non-government civilian contacts between Taiwan and the Chinese mainland were allowed.

In politics, the Taiwan government has long promoted local self-government. Beginning in 1950, all the chief executive and representative bodies under the provincial level were directly elected by the people, and in 1951, 16 county and 5 city governments and councils were established. In June 1959, the first Taiwan Provincial Assembly was established, extending political participation from the county to the provincial level.

Following the death of Chiang Kaishek in 1975, his son, Chiang Chingkuo, was elected president in 1978. It was under his rule that full democratization began, starting with the lifting of martial law in 1987 shortly before his death in early 1988. In fact, the first major opposition party, the Democratic Progressive Party (DPP), was formally established on September 28, 1986, marking the beginning of multiparty democracy in Taiwan. Chiang Chingkuo's successor, President Lee Tenghui, continued to reform the rigid political system that had been developed after decades of civil war and martial law. Under his administration, press freedoms were guaranteed, opposition political parties developed, visits to the mainland continued, and revisions of the constitution were encouraged.

These domestic political changes were closely intertwined with Taiwan's experience in the international arena. After the withdrawal of the government to Taiwan and the establishment of the People's Republic of China (PRC) on the mainland, diplomatic competition emerged between the two rivals. In 1971, supported by most of the newly independent states, the PRC succeeded in gaining admission to the United Nations General Assembly, and the ROC walked out. Since then, most of the remaining U.N. members have switched their ties from Taipei to Beijing. A low point was reached at the end of the 1970s, when the United States was the last major power to sever diplomatic ties. The U.S. has nonetheless continued economic ties and sold defensive military equipment to Taiwan in accordance with the Taiwan Relations Act of 1979.

Until 1987, Taiwan remained under martial law. At that time, opposing political parties were banned, publishing and the media were restricted, and relations with the mainland forbidden. However, religious and business activities were essentially free, and citizens regularly traveled around the island and the world. This policy was adopted because of the continued military threat from the Chinese mainland. As Taiwan prospered economically and the mainland undertook radical reforms and began to open up to the outside world, reasons for martial law were no longer seen as valid. On November 2, 1987, Taiwan officially permitted its citizens to visit relatives on the Chinese mainland. Since then, cross-strait ties have grown, and by the late 1990s Taiwan residents were making millions of trips, including visits to relatives, tourism, and scholarly, cultural, and sports exchanges. The number of trips made by mainland Chinese to Taiwan for cultural and educational activities has totaled more than 34,000.

In February 1991, the semi-private Straits Exchange Foundation (SEF) was set up to deal with matters arising from contact between people from both sides of the Straits. Its mainland counterpart, the Association for Relations Across the Taiwan Straits (ARATS), was established ten months later.

These organizations have met intermittently to discuss matters of a technical or business nature across the Straits, such as the repatriation of hijackers and illegal entrants, and solutions for fishing disputes.

CHAPTER 20

CHINA IN THE 21ST CENTURY

Viewed at the dawn of the 21st century, China stands to become one of the world's most powerful and dominating nations. Throughout the last century, China emerged as a world superpower and is predicted to build on this success throughout the course of the present century. China's military strength, international status, and economic development have all helped to distinguish it from the rest of the world. China is a unique country with strong customs and values, and an extremely fast-growing economy. All the nations in the world will have to take notice of China in the 21st century or risk being surpassed by this world-dominating country.

20.1   MILITARY STRENGTH

Today China is rapidly transforming into something new and unrecognizable. China is becoming one of the most powerful nations in the world not only from an economic standpoint, but also in terms of military strength. In order for a nation's military to be considered dominant, it must have the capability to not only defeat an enemy, but also to coerce and exercise influence over others. In recent times, China has proven its ability to do just this. The People's Republic of China has been seen by many as an economic powerhouse with the world's largest standing military—with the potential to translate economic power into military supremacy. Since 1949, the embodiment of this military force has been the People's Liberation Army (PLA).

The PLA is a major force in the Chinese economy, a potential participant in its politics, and a growing cause of concern to other nations in Asia. The PLA is somewhat less than twice the size of the United States military. It has a standing armed force of 2.8 million active soldiers that spans the army, navy, and air force. Approximately 1 million reservists and about 15 million militia back it up. With a population of 1.3 billion people, China also has the manpower reserve of another 200 million males in shape for military service at anytime. Not only does China have a wealth of manpower, it also has a great deal of nuclear power. It has enough megatonnage, missiles, and bombers to hit the United States, Europe, its Asian neighbors, and Russia. Domestically, the PLA has long sustained the Chinese Communist Party in power, which has been the main source that has enforced and maintained internal security. Regionally and internationally, the modernization and expansion of China's military has had great effects on the balance of power, has served as a source of concern to many nations, and has stimulated defense development in neighboring countries.

In order for its armed forces to thrive and expand, China has continued to rely heavily on reserved military funds. China's armed forces and the military budget that supports them are among the world's largest, and the budget has been constantly increasing at a rapid pace. The official budget now stands at just under US $15 billion per year; however, this military budget, passed annually by the National People's Congress, is an insufficient estimate because it only accounts for a portion of the revenues available to the PLA. Through these funds, China's military has been able to continuously improve, grow, and modernize.

The PLA has been progressively expanding even though in recent times China has been enjoying an unprecedented period of peace and absence of direct external military pressure. In the beginning of the 21st century, China seemingly faces no immediate external military threat to its national security and its borders continue to be peaceful. The Soviet threat has disappeared and relations with Russia are the best they have been in nearly half a century. Also, China has established diplomatic relations with most of its neighbors for the first time in its modern history. China's impressive economic growth and steady military modernization have contributed to its sense of assurance and security.

Even though China is in a period of peace, the PLA's view of the world is by no means relaxed. The PLA is aware of the problems that could arise in the future, and it continues to strive to stay ahead of these concerns. Some of these concerns include North Korea's instability and unpredictability, which impinges directly on Chinese security, and India's military capabilities and attainment of nuclear weapons, which have increased the presence of a new potential threat on China's southern borders. In addition, China's maritime claims in the East and South China Seas remain as potential conflict zones. Political tensions with Taiwan constantly have the potential to escalate to a military level. The most important concern, however, is the continuous strained relations with Japan and the United States. Although these problems may arise in the future, China is confident that its military strength will be ready.

Overall, China is moving toward military supremacy. Its economic and military strength have grown a great deal in recent years, and are projected to continue to grow significantly in the coming decades. Most observers of Asian international politics agree that the strategic direction and military position of China will be key factors in determining regional stability and security in the 21st century.

20.2 INTERNATIONAL STATUS

International relations and foreign policy have also become increasingly important to China in recent times. Since the end of the 20th century, China has begun to immensely expand trade and investment, which have created new links to the outside world. International relations and foreign policies will become vital issues for China if it wants to continue to work towards world dominance. However, the fact that China wants to grow in the world does not mean that it will abandon its ways and beliefs and adopt Western models and philosophy. China conducts business based on models developed from its own culture. For example, Chinese culture is based on the importance of rituals and ceremonies, and so is Chinese business. Decision-making and negotiating tactics differ from those of the West, causing misunderstanding and tension, which lead to difficulties in developing successful business and international relations.

Even though China believes strongly in its own values and customs, it is beginning to realize the importance of the Western powers and their influence. During 2001, two major events occurred in China that represented its desire to be accepted by the rest of the world. In July 2001, Beijing was awarded the

2008 Summer Olympic Games. This in fact was an enormous achievement for the world's most populous nation, since it signified China's favorable international relations and status. One of the most important benefits achieved from hosting the Olympics is the opportunity to show off your particular city and country to the rest of the world. The fact that Beijing has won this bid has allowed China a chance to step onto the world stage for the first time in a positive light. Many Chinese citizens consider hosting the Olympics as an honor worthy of enhancing national pride, and as a visible sign that China has overcome its "century of humiliation" and that it is truly a part of the community of nations. It will break down the barriers and be more amenable to communication and influence from the outside world.

The second event occurred in November 2001 when China finally joined the World Trade Organization (WTO), after a lengthy fight for acceptance. China's entry into the WTO will make China even more open. Both foreign investment and foreign trade are expected to increase a great deal. Trade will also increase in both directions. Chinese tariffs will be lowered and Chinese goods will have better access to world markets. The Chinese understand that in the coming years it will be closely watched by the world, so it must remain on its best behavior and cooperate to reap the overall benefits and solidify its international position.

In recent years, China has begun to make great strides in international relations and diplomatic work. In 2002, Sino-American relations were being gradually restored after difficulties in the first half of that year, and leaders of the two countries had reached a compromise on the development of bi-lateral relations. The Sino-Russian Good-Neighborly Treaty of Friendship and Cooperation signed between leaders of China and Russia in 2000 had laid the legal foundation for the development of mutual long-term friendship. Sino-European relations witnessed smooth development and entered a new era of all-around cooperation. Lastly, Sino-Japanese relations, while experiencing some ups and downs in recent times, returned to normal through joint efforts, and through the spirit of learning from history and confidently facing the future. China has started to make great efforts to open up to the outside world and enhance its international status.

20.3 ECONOMIC DEVELOPMENT

In the 21st century, China is also expected to become increasingly important as an economic power. China in fact has one of the world's fastest growing economies and there are those who predict that at its current rate of growth, China will be the world's largest economy by 2040, surpassing Japan and the United States. Today's economy in China is constantly evolving and is described as "socialism with Chinese characteristics." The economy in China is divided into three sectors, which include the state-owned sector, collective sector, and private sector. The government is still an important player in the Chinese economy, with about 60,000 state-owned industrial enterprises, which employ a workforce approaching 30 million. However, in recent years the trend has been moving towards private enterprises.

Some major factors in China's economic development include favorable international relations, acceptance into the World Trade Organization, and the adoption of an open door policy. By becoming a member of the WTO, China makes progress in freeing the Chinese economy from government control. The Open Door Policy is an essential element of economic progress and development. It encourages foreign investment and promotes foreign trade. Foreign investment has provided capital, new technology, managerial skills, and training for labor in China. It has introduced modern managerial systems, business practices, and legal frameworks for conducting business transactions that will ultimately help with economic development. It has also helped to provide competition in the domestic market, which has forced domestic enterprises to become more efficient. All these factors will in fact allow China to continue to increase its economic success.

The Olympic bid that Beijing won in July 2001 will not only help international relations and status, but it will also stimulate a great deal of economic development. According to the International Olympic Committee (IOC), the winner of the bid for the Olympics is guaranteed at least $1.2 billion for the sale of television rights and sponsorships. Therefore, when Beijing was named the winner, China knew that the Games would stimulate China's economy and accelerate reforms over the next seven years. The bid will also launch one of the county's largest building projects since the construction of the Great Wall began in the third century BC. The economic effects of the Olympics not only impact companies that are specifically in China, but also multinational corporations. The investments that these multinational companies will make will have a significant impact on China's economy as a whole.

Even though the economy in China has been improving over the years, it still has its share of problems that may hinder some economic developments. For instance, the state sector is in trouble. So serious is its deterioration that many argue that a political and economic crisis will result if it is not immediately and effectively addressed. Another concern is the unemployment problem. There are simply not enough jobs available to absorb the surplus of labor. Despite these problems, China is optimistic that its economy will continue to prosper and grow in the coming years.

Thus, as Lee Kuan Yew, the former Prime Minister of Singapore puts it, "China is not just another player. It is the biggest player in the history of man."

During the first half of the 21st century, China will increasingly emerge as a superpower in every sense — economically, politically, militarily, culturally, and technologically. Economists predict that China will be powerful enough internationally to become a rule setter, not just a rule follower. However, in order for China to evolve into this world superpower, it will need to deal more openly with the outside world. As the past twenty years of Chinese history have proven, once the barriers are lifted, there is no going back to old ways.

Provincial Map of Modern Day China

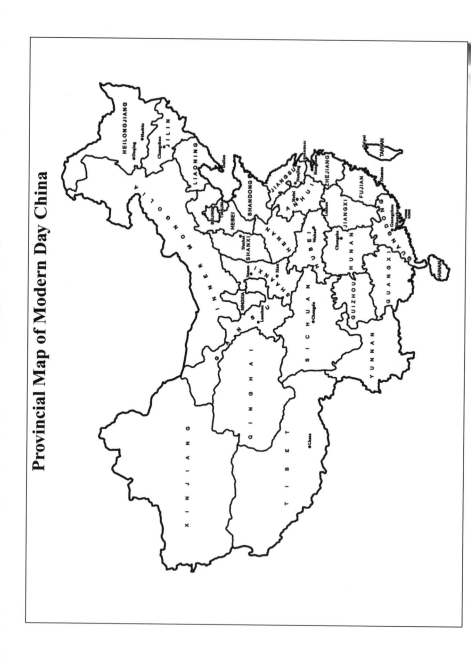

CHRONOLOGY OF MODERN CHINESE HISTORY

1839 - 1842	The Opium War Takes place between China and Great Britain.
August 24, 1842	The Opium War ends with the signing of the Treaty of Nanjing.
1851-1864	Hong Xiuquan begins the Taiping Uprising, leading to the founding of the Taiping Heavenly Kingdom in Nanjing in 1853. The Heavenly Kingdom falls on July 19, 1864.
1861-1895	China launches the Self-Strenthening Movement in an effort to modernize the country.
1879	Japan's annexation of the Ryukyu Kingdom takes place. China is alarmed by Japan's action

1894-1895	China's war with Japan over Korea occurs. China is defeated by Japan and forced to sign the Treaty of Shimonoseki, thereby ceding Taiwan to Japan.
1894	Dr. Sun Yatsen organizes the revolutionary Revive China Society.
1898	The Hunderd Day Reform takes place but fails. Kang Youwei and Liang Qichao flee to Japan.
1905	Dr. Sun Yatsen organizes the Chinese United League in Japan, and begins to stage military uprisings against the Qing dynasty.
October 10, 1911	Wuchang Uprising takes place.
1912	The Republic of China is established in Nanjing, but Yuan Shikai is elected provisional president on February 15 following the emperor's abdication.
June 6, 1916	Yuan Shikai dies and warlordism begins in China.
May 4, 1919	The May 4th Incident occurs.
July 23-31, 1921	The Chinese Communist Party is formed.
1923-1927	Dr. Sun Yatsen's Guangzhou government forms an alliance with the Soviet Union, and also admits the Chinese Communists into the Guomintang (Chinese Nationalist Party).

May 3, 1924	The Huangpu Military Academy is founded, with Chiang Kaishek appointed as its principal.
1926	The Northern Expedition to wipe out the warlords in China begins.
April 12, 1927	Chaing Kaishek orders the purge of Communists in Shanghai.
October 1928	Chaing Kaishek is elected president after having re-unified China.
1928-1934	Mao Zedong and the Chinese Communists regroup in Jinggangshan, and the Jiangxi Soviet Republic is established in 1931.
1931-1934	Chaing Kaishek launches five extermination campaigns against the Chinese Communists, forcing them to undertake the 6,000-mile Long March to Yan'an.
Sept. 18, 1931	Japan attacks Manchuria.
Dec. 12, 1936	The Xi'an Incident occurs.
July 7, 1937	Japan attacks China Proper. The Marco Polo Bridge Incident occurs.
Aug. 14, 1945	Japan surrenders
1945-1949	The Civil War takes place, leading to the Communist victory on the Mainland, and the Nationalist retreat to the island of Taiwan

Oct. 1, 1949	The People's Republic of China is founded by Mao.
1953	The First Five-Year Plan officially begins.
1956-1957	The Hundred Flowers Campaign takes place, which ends with the Anti-Rightist Campaign against intellectual dissidents.
1958	The Great Leap Forward begins, which is a part of the Three Red Banner policy (the Great Leap Forward, the General Line, and the People's Communes).
April 27, 1959	Liu Shaoqi is elected state chairman, thus beginning his feud with Mao who is still party chairman.
1962-1965	The Socialist Education Movement takes place.
1966-1969	Mao leads the Great Proletarian Cultural Revolution. Liu is under house arrest. Defense Minister Lin Biao is named Mao's successor.
Sept. 13, 1971	Lin Biao dies in a plane crash after an alleged coup attempt.
April 5, 1975	Chiang Kaishek dies in Taiwan.
1976	Zhou Enlai dies (Jan. 8), Hua Guofeng succeeds as premier. Mao also dies (Sept. 9), leading to the arrest of Jiang Qing and her three close associates (Gang of Four). Deng Xiaoping begins to reappear in public.

1979	The Open Door Policy and economic reform begin to take shape.
1980	Zhao Ziyang and Hu Yaobang are elected to the Politboro.
1980s	The Special Economic Zones are being set up.
April 15, 1989	Hu Yaobang dies.
June 3-4, 1989	The Tiananmen Square Incident occurs — killing hundreds of demonstrators — and Zhao Ziyang is removed from all of his posts. Jiang Zemin emerges as a national leader.
October 1992	The plan of a "socialist market economic system" is introduced into China in order to ensure success in its future development.
March 27, 1993	Jiang Zemin is appointed president of the PRC.
Feb. 19, 1997	Deng Xiaoping dies at the age of 93.
July 1, 1997	China regains control of Hong Kong.
March 2000	The Nationalists lose the presidential election in Taiwan to the pro-independence Democratic Progressive Party.

July 1, 2001	Jiang Zemin presents his July 1 Speech, which includes the "Three Representatives Theory."
July 13, 2001	Beijing wins the bid to host the 2008 Summer Olympic Games.
Nov. 10, 2001	The World Trade Organization (WTO) accepts China as a member.

NOTES

NOTES